STAPLES FOR SUCCESS

FROM BUSINESS PLAN TO BILLION-DOLLAR BUSINESS IN JUST A DECADE

Edited by
Thomas G. Stemberg

KNOWLEDGE EXCHANGE
SANTA MONICA, CALIFORNIA

KEX CUSTOM

Knowledge Exchange, 1299 Ocean Avenue
Santa Monica, California 90401

Copyright © 1996 by Staples, Inc.
All rights reserved

Printed in the United States of America

CONTENTS

1. The Staples Concept: Anatomy of the Big Idea 1

2. Entering the World of "Subject To" Hiring 11

3. Raising Money: Angels and Mere Mortals 25

4. Of Landlords and Real Estate 41

5. Competition: Friend and Foe 55

6. New York and Other Foreign Cities 71

7. Race of the Retailers 89

8. The Price of Success: Glory and Infamy 97

9. Mistakes: Real and Imagined..................115

10. Getting Bigger: Turning Weaknesses into Strengths..........125

11. Lessons Learned: A Personal Journey 139

Index 146

1 THE STAPLES CONCEPT: ANATOMY OF THE BIG IDEA

Most people adore the fairy-tale version of Staples' beginnings. Tom Stemberg, a 36-year-old Harvard Business School graduate who had recently been fired from his job as president of a First National Supermarkets division, was working on a business plan in his West Hartford, Connecticut, home in the summer of 1985. When he began to print out spreadsheets—dozens of them—his printer ribbon broke. No problem. He'd just scoot down to Plimpton's stationery store. It was a Friday, but Plimpton's was closed because it was the Fourth of July weekend. The nearest computer store? Also closed. "Okay," thought Stemberg, "I'll run up to BJ's Wholesale Club, north of Hartford. BJ's was open. But with an inventory of only 100 office supply items, it didn't have his ribbon. Then, wham! A vision blindsided Stemberg: What the world needed was a superstore selling nothing but office supplies at great prices.

The incident is true, but it's hardly the real story of how a revolutionary idea evolved. The peculiar alchemy that spurred a bright, out-of-work executive to create a store that would revolutionize the way people buy paper clips and tape included these unpromising ingredients: unglamorous products, unwilling customers, and skeptical suppliers. What turned those elements into a $3 billion company in a $100 billion industry? What was it about Staples that sparked a parade of well-heeled imitators across the country? How did Staples maintain its role as an industry leader?

Not every business has the potential to grow 50 percent a year. But every business owner can learn from the Staples story. The lessons aren't ones you'll find in Harvard Business School case studies. But they have been road tested by one of the most successful start-up companies in the country, contending with some of the most demanding business conditions anywhere.

The truth is that the big idea was years in the making. Like most inventions, the concept for an office supplies superstore was the result of a number of events and personalities coming together bit by bit. Clearly, Stemberg himself was the alchemist. The son of a Newark, New Jersey, restaurateur and caterer, Stemberg had established himself as an innovator in the staid supermarket industry within a decade of graduating from Harvard Business School in 1973. At Star Markets, a Boston-based unit of Jewel Companies in Chicago, Stemberg developed and launched the first line of unbranded—or "generic"—foods sold in the country. The move was brash and unprecedented in the food industry. Old hands—some of them at Jewel—predicted failure. But consumers loved it. Sales of the onetime laggard in the Boston area soared, and by 1982, Star tied Purity Supreme, a fierce local competitor, for first place.

That experience laid the foundation for Staples in two important ways. First, it earned Stemberg the respect of Leo Kahn, the flinty chief executive of Purity Supreme who built his company into Boston's highest-volume food retailer largely because he introduced warehouse food stores to New England. "He was very strong and capable," remembers Kahn. "He pushed generics very hard though my company and other companies disagreed with the concept." Second, it confirmed for Stemberg the power of identifying and satisfying a customer's need, a lesson that had been drummed into him at Harvard. In this case, consumers' desire for low grocery bills was especially strong, because double-digit inflation was driving food prices higher month by month.

First National Supermarkets, Stemberg's next corporate home, gave him hands-on experience with another key component: warehouse selling. As president of the company's loss-riddled Edwards-Finast division, Stemberg once again focused on fulfilling customers' need for low prices, but this time he changed the setting. Instead of offering a few aisles of low-priced generics, he created gigantic stores carrying Edwards-Finast brand products. The stores' rock-bottom prices were the result of the rock-bottom costs associated with buying in volume and operating a no-frills store.

If the owners of First National Supermarkets had not put the company up for sale, Stemberg might still be in the

TOM STEMBERG

"A superstore was the answer because you had to create something with a cost structure that enables you to keep prices low. There's a reason why nobody had low prices in office supplies. If you sold the stuff the way the old guys did it—which is to buy in small lots and try to deliver it by your own trucks and so forth—it's obvious why stationers needed high prices to support those costs. The supermarket approach, with which I was familiar, seemed like a logical way to bring efficiency into the picture. Toys "R" Us was a supermarket. Home Depot was a supermarket, basically, for bigger, bulkier goods, but essentially a supermarket. My aim was to take the same approach and satisfy customers with lower prices."

supermarket industry. Instead, in anticipation of the sale, First National fired Stemberg in December of 1985. He was outraged—and scared. He had a two-year old son and a household to support. Would he be able to get another job in the industry with this blot on his record? Fortunately, he had advantages that softened the blow. First National would pay his salary for a year, and he was able to tap the expertise of one-time competitor, Leo Kahn. The 68-year-old had sold his supermarket chain to Supermarkets General in 1984 for $80 million and was frustrated in his search for a new business opportunity. Upon hearing that Stemberg had been fired, Kahn's first reaction was surprise. His second: "I had respect for him. I wanted to see if we could go in together on a new venture." Together they began to search for retailing opportunities.

But Stemberg was also intrigued by questions raised by Walter Salmon, a friend and Harvard Business School professor: Why try to excel in an industry replete with up-to-date competitors? Why not start your own business, a business that brings the modern techniques of distribution used by supermarkets to a nonfood product? posited Salmon. The questions struck a chord. Stemberg's experiences at Star and Edwards-Finast had given him a taste for shaking up the status quo. In his experience, boldness worked. This appetite for novelty allowed Stemberg to look for a chance to deploy proven business strategies (low prices and warehouse selling) in a new arena. It prompted him to look outside the mainstream. And so ordinary details—hardly noticeable to most businesspeople—leapt out at him.

The defining moment came on a Saturday afternoon in January of 1985. Makro, a struggling group of warehouse-style stores owned by two European companies, had been wooing Stemberg to become CEO of its U.S. operation. Stemberg, a devoted fan of Harvard's basketball team, decided to tour one of Makro's stores in Langhorne, Pennsylvania, after attending a game in nearby Princeton. With Harvard victorious for the first time in 25 years, Stemberg was exhilarated as he entered the store that afternoon. Within minutes he knew the store wouldn't work in the U.S. It was gigantic and the prices were good. But the store concept was a mess. Instead of focusing on a single type of product, Makro had everything: apparel, food, electronics, toys. Nevertheless one detail caught his eye. "Makro's office supplies were flying off the shelves," recalls Stemberg. "That was the day the idea formed: could we create a Toys "R" Us for office supplies?"

Real-Life Lesson

Groundbreaking business ideas don't spring full-blown into entrepreneurs' brains. *It's a myth perpetuated in magazines and books, and even by entrepreneurs. In hindsight, a business' creation looks preordained. But in fact, the most creative ideas spring from long and intense experience with the components of the yet-to-be-created business. If Stemberg had not mastered the fundamentals—low pricing and warehouse-style selling—he would have never spotted the chance to use those selling techniques in office supplies.*

Low Prices:
A Solution to a Problem Nobody Has?

"Leo, look. For you this is an interesting investment. For me, it's my life. We've got to go study this."

Stemberg was gratified by Kahn's enthusiasm for the office supplies superstore concept. Bob Nakasone, president of Toys "R" Us and a friend from Stemberg's Jewel days, was also gung ho. But Stemberg, intensely analytical, would not be satisfied until he had exhaustively researched the idea.

He started by simply interviewing every small business owner he knew: his typist, his dry cleaner, his lawyer, his doctor. "What do you spend on office supplies?" he asked. Nobody knew. They'd guess. So he pressed harder. One of his friends, Coleman Levy, a lawyer in Farmington, Connecticut, told Stemberg that his annual tab for office supplies was about $10,000, or $200 per employee. Appealing to his frugal nature, Stemberg challenged Levy to check his invoices. Together they pawed through dozens of invoices. "We discovered office supplies were actually costing Levy $1,000 per employee. He was spending $50,000 a year," recalls Stemberg. Levy was aghast.

"Once you explain to people how badly they're getting ripped off, and how much money is involved, you can actually create demand for low prices," says Stemberg. "But it is not an easy sell because they don't realize they have a problem. They do have a problem—they just don't know they have a problem." It was a fascinating lesson—but a puzzle. If small business owners believed their office supply expenses were negligible, they'd hardly be enticed by low prices.

The next question to answer: what kind of bargain would Staples be able to offer small business owners? To figure out what buyers of copier paper, paper clips, and other office supplies were currently paying, Stemberg posed as a potential customer of Boise Cascade and other dealers. First, he called on behalf of Ivy Satellite Network, a small company he owned that broadcasted events of Ivy League schools to alumni around the world. Boise Cascade, which had great prices, couldn't be bothered with sending a catalogue to Ivy Satellite, much less call on the tiny company.

Next, he called Boise back, this time representing the 100-person office of Fred Alper, a food broker friend in Boston. This time Boise was happy to trot out to Alper's office, and Stemberg was astonished by what they offered. A Bic pen from Boise would cost Alper just 85 cents. At the mom-and-pop stationery store that poor Ivy Satellite was forced to use, the price was $3.68. Discounts from large dealers just weren't available to 20-person companies. "The most I could ever talk a dealer into—when I told him Ivy was going to be the next ESPN—was a 20 percent discount," says Stemberg, with a laugh.

Further research confirmed Stemberg's discovery. Small companies were paying through the nose, while large companies could command huge discounts off the list price. An aggressive office manager of a company with 1000 or more white-collar workers could obtain discounts of up to 50 percent from dealers. Small businesses with only 10 to 20 employees, on the other hand, were lucky to get a 10 percent discount. They often paid full price.

This pricing gap was tremendously relevant information. Stemberg could visualize the impact Staples' prices would have upon his future customers. Imagine customer reaction, he wrote in his business plan during the summer of 1985, when confronting signs like these:

WHILE YOU WERE OUT PADS
List Price $4.32
STAPLES' PRICE $1.39

LIQUID PAPER
List Price $1.49
STAPLES' PRICE $ .89

Stemberg figured he'd be able to save small companies $500 or more for each employee annually. And though they had been ignored, small companies could fuel Staples' growth indefinitely. In total, small companies buy more office products than large companies. Even 10 years ago, it was clear that small companies were in ascendancy. Out of 11 million businesses in the country in 1985, 10.8 million were small businesses. John Naisbitt's *Megatrends,* which had recently been published, predicted that the transformation of the U.S. manufacturing economy into a service economy would spawn an even greater proliferation of small businesses.

Best of all, the market for office supplies was huge—$85 billion—and already growing rapidly. Total sales of paper goods, clips, staples, and other basic supplies had grown at a 12.7 percent annual rate from 1978 to 1983, and even faster—16.8 percent—in 1983 and 1984. Furniture and equipment, products that Stemberg also viewed as integral elements of his future stores, had similarly fast growth rates.

The more Stemberg uncovered about the trade, the more the Staples concept looked like a slam dunk. But there was one problem that kept him up at night: Everything about his idea revolved around the allure of low prices, but low prices simply did not matter much to his target customers. In companies with 20 to 99 employees, an office or purchasing manager was in charge of ordering supplies and remarkably indifferent to how much they cost. Such employees rarely were praised for saving money because the expense was usually such a small portion of the company's revenues. On the other hand, office managers risked the wrath of everyone in the company if its stock of pens, receipt pads, and other supplies ran out. Though smaller companies, with 20 or fewer employees, were far more price-conscious, they liked the convenience of having supplies delivered or shopping at a two-doors-away stationer. To succeed, Stemberg couldn't just offer low prices and vast selection. He would have to change the behavior of businesses altogether.

Very few who knew the industry believed it could be done. Buying supplies in stores was inconvenient, according to Ralph Margolius of Allied Office Supply in Norfolk,

Excerpt from Stemberg's 1985 Business Plan

"The greatest challenge STAPLES faces is to change the behavior of office products consumers. In particular those businesses that currently have their office supplies delivered must be convinced to send someone out to pick them up. Among small white-collar business, which constitute STAPLES' primary market, the challenge is greatly reduced because such businesses frequently send a designated employee to visit a dealer's storefront or a mass market channel to pick up supplies. Whatever the severity of the challenge, a primary goal of STAPLES' management will be to communicate the benefits of its new way of procuring office supplies. . . . Since STAPLES' ability to master this challenge will be the key to its success, management is prepared to invest heavily in marketing."

Virginia. In an office products trade journal, he stated, "My customers have noted that they have to devote a lot of time to shop, locate items, load and transport, and stand in long lines at the check-out counters." And Wallace Pellerin of Texan Business Products in Austin, Texas, practically wrote off customers' interest in low prices saying, "I sell product knowledge, service, . . . and I'm not going to worry about customers who want to save a dime!"

Real-Life Lesson

The single best thing you can do to make your business succeed—at any point in time—is to focus on the customer. *This idea has been so widely propounded that it has become trite. The key to making it a fresh exercise is to think about the customer's point of view on both an impersonal and a personal level. If Stemberg had simply come up with his idea for a product—a Toys "R" Us for office supplies—and proceeded to implement the idea, he might have failed. By researching customers' needs and behavior objectively he discovered the huge price disparity between large and small businesses. By listening to the customers' personal points of view, he learned that many did not know they were overpaying and others did not really care. Daunting as this knowledge might have been, it forced Stemberg to realize early on that Staples' success or failure would largely be contingent on how well it could change customers' perception and behavior.*

2 ENTERING THE WORLD OF "SUBJECT TO" HIRING

While it's true that powerful ideas draw resources like magnets, it's not necessarily true that the resources show up at the right time. Stemberg faced all the Catch-22s familiar to most start-ups. In order to attract managers to his new venture, he needed capital. In order to draw venture capital, he needed to be able to demonstrate that he had an able management team. Suppliers did not want to ship products to Staples, of course, unless Stemberg could prove he could pay for them and had a store to put them in. Landlords were not interested in leasing store space to a start-up if it didn't have a strong balance sheet and the confidence of its suppliers . . . and round and round it went.

"The first venture capitalist I talked to said, 'I'm not going to finance this. There's no management team,'" recalls Stemberg. "So then you go to a management team and they say, 'Do you have any money?' Everyone's participation is subject to something else. You live in a world of 'subject to.'"

The only way to put the pieces of the puzzle together was to work on all fronts simultaneously. Stemberg began courting his future employees even before he had firm commitments from venture capitalists. It quickly became clear that even with money behind Staples, Stemberg would only be able to draw on managers who fit into certain categories.

"You don't get the smooth corporate executive who's on his way up and about to take his career to the moon," says Stemberg. The executives who'd be willing to take a flier on a start-up were inexperienced, experienced but with limited skills, or unhappy with their employer.

Ian Patrick, the executive who was supposed to become Staples' very first employee, was a prime example of the difficulties Stemberg faced in hiring. From Stemberg's point of view, Patrick had everything. A veteran of Xerox, Patrick had moved onto Boise Cascade and built up its Washington, D.C., operation from a two-person sales unit generating $1 million in revenues to a $12 million business in just four years. Beyond his obvious skills as a salesman and manager, Patrick would offer Staples a vital connection to Boise, the most important vendor in the office products industry. Patrick, whose interest in joining Staples was strong enough that Stemberg included him in his original business plan, had a keen attraction to the Staples concept. But when it came time to actually make such a move, he declined. It was hard to choose an unproven start-up over a successful career in a preeminent company.

Using a headhunter, Stemberg approached dozens of executives, painting his vision of Staples' future at 6:30 in the morning over scrambled eggs and bacon at Boston's Charles Hotel or the Atrium in Harvard Square, or over cheeseburgers at the Harvard Club. As the summer of 1985 drew to a close, it became clear that Stemberg's best bets would be people who were part of the supermarket industry and had some prior connection to him—people who shared his outlook would be less likely to see Staples as a huge risk. One of them was Myra Hart, an executive at Star Markets. A former schoolteacher who had graduated from Harvard Business School at age 37, Hart had interviewed with Stemberg at Star and gone through the same training program that he had. Though she was a single mother with two kids in college, she had little fear about joining Stemberg. "Once I saw the business plan, I knew it was almost a sure winner. The idea of selling office products the way food was sold made complete sense. It was clear there wouldn't be any difficulty in making that plan come to life," she says.

Another key hire, 49-year-old Bob Leombruno, also had a special appreciation for Stemberg's concept. Leombruno had successfully helped bring Mammoth Mart, a failed retail operation, out of bankruptcy and into the black for a group of investors. "I was convinced that it would work from day one," remembers Leombruno. Paul Korian, a gregarious 39-year-old who was running the East Coast merchandising operation of Osco Drug (a drugstore chain that is currently a division of American Stores) jumped to Staples primarily for personal reasons. Osco was in the process of moving its managers to Chicago and Korian, a longtime Boston dweller, did not want to move. Korian filled the role intended for Ian Patrick: getting merchandise into Staples' stores.

The fundamental attraction of joining Staples was the chance to get rich. Anyone turned on by the idea of overhauling the distribution of stationery, Post-It notes, Bic pens, and other supplies to business customers was someone who saw the vast money machine that could be created by a chain of Staples. They would want a piece of the business, and Stemberg had no qualms about giving them one.

"It's simple," he explains. "The pitch was this: 'I'm going to give you a big chunk of stock in this thing. This is your chance. We're all going to work our tails off. We're going to work crazy hours. But here you'll be part of a retailing revolution. If you own 2 percent of the company and it gets to be worth $100 million, you're going to make $2 million.'" Though each member of Staples' first management team negotiated different stakes for themselves, within months of beginning the company Stemberg adjusted their shares so that each owned 250,000 shares out of the 10 million outstanding—2.5 percent of the company.

Stemberg's "share the spoils" philosophy wasn't pure generosity. It was pragmatic. Sharing stock ownership unifies self-interest with the company's best interest. Instead of asking whether a decision will hurt his chance for promotion, or her importance within the company, the ultimate measure becomes, How will this affect the company's success?

Also, Stemberg had little to offer besides stock. Venture capitalists had made it clear that they expected Stemberg and his team to take 33 percent pay cuts. (Because they're putting up the money, venture capitalists impose such financial duress to ensure that an entrepreneur and his managers will work like maniacs to make a success out of a new venture.) Stemberg, who had been earning $240,000 at First National Supermarkets, was required to cut his pay to $170,000. Myra Hart says, "I don't think Tom could have gotten the employees he did if he hadn't offered an equity stake. Remember, when we got our stock it was worthless. We took a cut in income and invested at least twice as much labor as we would have in our previous jobs."

Stemberg was forced to recover from some hiring mistakes immediately. Because Staples' success was dependent on changing the buying habits of its target audience, Stemberg knew that he had to find a marketing professional before venture capitalists would commit their funds. He hired an advertising executive at Mintz and Hoke Advertising, in Avon, Connecticut, whose team had designed the advertising campaign that helped turn around Stemberg's Edwards-Finast division. But the executive's expertise was in broadcast advertising. What Staples needed was someone who could pull customers into the store with specials, direct mail campaigns, and promotions. Within a few weeks of Staples' corporate launch, Stemberg, Hart, Korian and Leombruno were working feverish 70-hour weeks when they noticed the new marketing manager had withdrawn to his office to work on a big project. The mysterious work-in-progress turned out to be hand-drawn invitations to his own upcoming housewarming party. Shortly thereafter, he left the company.

Stemberg cast about for someone to fill the crucial marketing function and found Todd Krasnow, a 28-year-old Harvard Business School graduate working, once again, at Star Markets. It was a gamble. Though Krasnow was bright and had worked for Hart, he was green. Over the board's strenuous objections, Stemberg hired Krasnow. "I had spent four years bagging groceries, stocking shelves, cutting meat, dealing with customers, managing store departments," says Krasnow. "It was a very, very solid base in retailing and so when Tom called, it was perfect for me. I wasn't walking away from anything that was particularly special."

Real-Life Lesson

A start-up has little to offer a well-positioned highly talented executive. *To get experienced executives you have to appeal to people whose background enables them to share your vision and who are unhappy with their current position. Hiring inexperienced people is a gamble, but one that may be worth taking. Krasnow, now executive vice president for sales and marketing, is still at Staples even though many of the experienced managers Stemberg originally hired are not. Either way, share the spoils of your company's future accomplishments.* "You want everybody there committed to the utmost degree to your ultimate success and you want a total alignment of goals," says Stemberg. "Letting your colleagues have an enlightened economic interest in your mutual success is a great way to run your business."

Getting Started: Creating Something Out of Nothing

Staples swung into operation in January of 1986 in a style befitting its no-frills theme. The corporate office was 5,000 square feet in an old mill building on California Street in Newton, Massachusetts. The space, owned by Leo Kahn, once housed the offices of Kings department stores and still contained a few pieces of office furniture dating from the 1950s. It hardly mattered to the tiny crew of five officers and two assistants. They were focused on a much more devilish issue: how to get the first Staples store opened in just four months. The group would meet every morning at about 7:00 A.M. in a session that could run from thirty minutes to two hours. Then everyone would go to work. Someone would dash out for sandwiches at lunchtime, and everyone would eat them together in Staples' shabby board room. The workday came to a close at 9:00 P.M. or 10:00 P.M., when everyone would stop by Stemberg's office and chat informally about the day's progress.

"That first year we all had our eyes on the goal, our heads down all the time," remembers Hart, who was in charge of getting the store location ready. "We were on a constant adrenaline rush. Everything we did was for the first time. We usually thought what we were doing was a good idea, but we weren't really sure it would work."

The pressure was enormous. Not only was the team of would-be retailers attempting to open a store in a remarkably short period of time, it was trying to meet that schedule for a monster store that no one had ever seen the likes of before. There was no template, no example to study in deciding their course of action. Another layer of difficulty: this store was only the first. According to Krasnow, "We had to be putting in place the capability to open one store

Myra Hart

"The building sat idle and had gone unrepaired and grown outdated. Everything was antiquated. We got buckets and rubber gloves and the first few days were spent washing and cleaning up. We couldn't sit down and even begin to operate until we did that. The furniture was second-hand—old steel desks and plastic chairs. It was spartan to say the least, but that was our intention. Our whole purpose was to say 'We save money and we save money in every sense.' It was a necessity but it was also part of our image."

after another, so you couldn't just do what was expedient. You had to think through a set of implications and decide how to build a system every step of the way."

One of the most worrisome projects fell to Leombruno, the chief financial officer. In addition to setting up the accounting system and reporting to venture capitalists about the fledgling company's expenditures and forecasts, he was in charge of buying and installing Staples' central and store computer systems. The technology would have a huge impact upon customers' actual shopping experience as well as the company's ability to operate efficiently. The computers had to be able to track customer purchases so that the company could reorder products. Hart also believed it was crucial that the store's cash registers be easy to operate so that any employee could use them, thus reducing the chance of check-out congestion. Stemberg wanted register receipts to indicate the list price of each item, as well as the much-lower Staples price, and the even-lower price for customers who became Staples "members." No system that met every requirement even existed at that point, so the group spent hours debating what to forego, and finally decided that price comparison was the most important feature. Larry Kennedy, a member of Staples' original management information systems team, fashioned the country's first system of cash registers that could assign three different prices to a particular store item.

At the same time, Leombruno scoured computer outlets and dealers to find IBM hardware at a 20 percent discount while still retaining IBM's technical support. One of the accounting firms, upon whom he had been depending to analyze systems, seemed to be billing lots of hours without reaching decisions. He released the firm and redoubled his efforts. During one marathon work session in February, he and Larry Kennedy and their staff worked 36 hours straight to install Staples' central computer system.

As head of merchandising, Korian's enormous task was to get suppliers to ship products to Staples' first store. It was one of the biggest hurdles the company faced. What Staples was proposing to the Esseltes, Gillettes, and International Papers of the world was nothing less than disrupting the distribution system of an entire industry. It would have been hard enough just to get such behemoths to ship to a new and unproven company. But Korian and Stemberg were also asking them to support a store that—if it were successful—would undercut and potentially demolish some of their best customers. "Our vision was to totally mess up the existing channel of distribution, so they were going to fight us very hard," points out Krasnow.

How did Staples pull it off? Any way it could. Just as in every other dimension of this start-up, friends and connections helped. For instance, Bessemer Securities, one of Staples' investors, owned Ampad, a manufacturer of paper pads. And even though Staples represented a threat to the industry, Stemberg made it a point to join the National Office Products Association. Though many in the industry would come to hate Staples—Krasnow recalls being spit on by stationers in the same elevator with him at a Chicago trade conference in 1987—the trade group itself could not treat Staples, one of its own members, as an enemy.

Stemberg and Korian wooed and cajoled in order to get suppliers on board. But what proved most effective in signing up most of them was their gutsy portrayal of the Staples vision and the powerhouse it would eventually become. At one now-legendary meeting at the International House of Pancakes where Korian had assembled dozens of small and large suppliers, Stemberg discussed Staples' substantial backing and how the store would be different from wholesale clubs, which at the time were scaring everyone associated with retailing. Staples would be big. Staples would succeed. The punchline was that if suppliers did not work with the little company now, they'd be sorry. "I'm going to be very loyal to those who stick their necks out for us. But it's going to cost you a lot more to get in later," Stemberg declared.

Tom Stemberg's Pitch to Suppliers

"You know, you suppliers are hearing a lot of malarkey from the boys throughout the industry. They're complaining that you shouldn't be selling us. The stationery wholesalers are saying you shouldn't be selling us. I want to tell you something. There are three kinds of people in this world. There are those who make things happen. There are those who observe what happens. And then there are those who wonder what happened. We're going to make something happen here. You have a chance to get in up front. Don't be one of those who wondered what happened. When this train leaves the station and this thing gets going, if you don't tell me you're part of it right now, somebody else will. And we're going to be very loyal to those people who leave on that first train with us."

Real-Life Lesson

Live reality, dream the dream. *Stemberg and his band of shirtsleeve managers had a daily diet of cognitive dissonance. The reality was that suppliers were digging in their heels, raising the specter of a store with empty shelves. The dream was that this store would not only be the first of many stores, but that Staples would grow big and profitable enough to become a public company—making all of them wealthy. Instead of being a handicap, this disparity between reality and vision was necessary to get the company going—and has continued to be a vital part of Staples' ethos.*

When Nobody Shows Up: The First Store

Staples snagged its first lease in Brighton, Massachusetts, but it was no coup. The site, situated between the Charles River on one side and the Massachusetts Turnpike on the other, was within sight of Boston housing projects and had failed a number of different retail incarnations. But the Staples team was pinning its hopes on two key features. The location was easily accessible and happened to sit smack in the middle of a high concentration of small businesses.

Myra Hart, however, had the unenviable task of turning the location into a proper store. The building had been added onto over a period of years and looked like an auto junkyard. The construction crew regularly unearthed old bumpers and wheels. But the most nerve-wracking chore was getting the store's occupancy permit. Boston had a labyrinthian process for obtaining permits from the Building Department that was further complicated by Staples not being familiar with local procedures. Hart patiently shepherded Staples' store plans through each of the five or

---

TOM STEMBERG

"All the time, when you hit those adversities, you've got to behave very rationally and deal with all the facts at hand. But in terms of the way you conduct yourself and the way you lead others, you've got to continue to dream the dream. You can't make it fiction. You can't make it full of falsehoods, because then you'll fail for sure. But you've got to see opportunity in the teeth of adversity and you have to seize on an opportunity and make it clear and paint it vividly for those around you, to help them get over the challenges."

---

six jurisdictions that had to approve them, repairing objections and resubmitting changes. It was dreary work that lasted for weeks.

Finally, one Friday in April, she got everything signed off and walked into a final bureaucrat's office to get the certificate of occupancy that was required in order for Staples to obtain insurance coverage. It was 4:00 in the afternoon and the city employee refused to give her the certificate. Worse, he said he was going on vacation the following week. "I was a little naive," says Hart now. "We didn't know about all the graft going on in the department." So instead of greasing the wheels, Hart yelled. Fortunately, after spending so many days hanging around, Hart had become familiar to many Building Department employees. One of them came over to ask Hart what was wrong and intervened on her behalf. She got Staples' first occupancy permit.

While Hart was perfecting the store's exterior, Krasnow and Stemberg were wrestling with the central risk of the entire Staples concept: how to get customers to change their behavior. Research showed that low prices were not going to attract small businesses. "There was tremendous resistance," explains Krasnow. "People said, 'Why in the world would I go to a stationery store to buy this stuff?' Because their preconceived image involved going into a 2,000-square-foot, unpleasant, dirty store that didn't have a lot of products and that had high prices. On top of that, they all said, 'I have salespeople call on me. They send me tickets to ball games. They send me flowers.' They liked that part of their job, and we were asking them to trade that for becoming a gopher!"

Despite such resistance, Staples opened its first store on May 1, 1986. The opening day, to which everybody that anyone at Staples knew had been invited, was a great success. On the second day, the store had only sixteen customers, and on the third day, about the same number. Krasnow decided to bribe customers to get them in. Advertising wouldn't work. It was expensive in the Boston market, especially with Staples' limited budget. So Krasnow paid twenty-five small business managers twenty dollars to shop in the store and tell him what they thought. "A week later we called them back. They had all taken the money, but hadn't come into the store. I was apoplectic," remembers Krasnow. Nine finally came in and gave Staples rave reviews.

That was the beginning of Staples' inventive marketing style. Krasnow continued to send out direct mail solicitations using information from publicly available databases. He'd "bribe" customers by mail, offering $20-off coupons or free copy paper. But instead of being content to get customers in the door, he devised a plan for refining his promotions. Once they came to the store to use the

TODD KRASNOW

"I lived a quarter of a mile from the office, it just so happened, and we worked from six in the morning until midnight. You could literally be there twenty-four hours a day, there was just so much to do.

There was no store like this in existence, so there was nothing with which to compare it. There was no example of how to display the product. Everything was in plain kraft paper or in boxes marked 'Stock keeping unit 7332, five hundred #10 envelopes, Gum/Win.' You can't sell that. So it was a real challenge to figure out how to sell these products. We spent a huge amount of time trying to figure it out. At first we didn't display the products, so every customer would have to open every box to find what they wanted. You'd end up with all these ripped boxes all over the place, which people then wouldn't buy."

coupons, Staples asked them to become "members," by filling out a card that would include vital statistics about the customers' companies. Now Staples could measure if it was getting a good return on its promotional efforts. "We might have concluded that for one-person offices, it isn't worth it to spend $20 to get them in the store," explains Krasnow. "On the other hand, for a 15-person office it might be worth spending $100." At the time, such database marketing was almost unheard of in retailing. Now, it's commonplace.

Real-Life Lesson

If standard marketing formulas don't work, invent your own. *There were no role models for Staples' store, so naturally there was no blueprint for how to reach customers. The key to Krasnow's solution was not only that he tried something different, but that he measured the results. His program would not have worked in a grocery store, because each customer doesn't spend enough to justify the cost of maintaining a database. But an office manager, on the other hand, might shell out hundreds of dollars during each visit.*

3 RAISING MONEY: ANGELS AND MERE MORTALS

When Bob Reilly, a 44-year-old partner at the Boston-based investment bank Downer & Co., sat down to chat with Stemberg on a spring day in 1985, he was taken aback. He had agreed to meet with Stemberg as a favor to a friend. Stemberg was young, had a terrific résumé, but spoke in a rapid murmur that Reilly at first could barely decipher. Though Stemberg would later prove to be an adept communicator in front of live audiences and television cameras, at this meeting he spoke in a "telegraphic mumble," remembers Reilly, with a laugh.

It was an inauspicious beginning for a successful relationship that would prove critical to Stemberg's capital-raising efforts. In hindsight, Stemberg's encounter with Reilly looks like simple good luck. But it wasn't. It was a prime example of Stemberg's ability to choose the best resources for solving the problems he faced.

Reilly would become the money hub for Staples. When they had first met, Stemberg was still intent upon buying a supermarket chain. Downer, which specialized in U.S. acquisitions for European companies, scouted around for supermarkets and quickly discovered that the available chains were either too big, or too expensive, for Stemberg. It didn't matter though, because Stemberg had been overtaken by the idea for an office supplies superstore.

But he had a money quandary. Not the one most entrepreneurs confront—which is how to get capital. Stemberg's difficulty was how to get capital from the right places. Leo Kahn and Danny Coven, his financial advisor, had told Stemberg that they were willing to finance the whole company. Most businessmen would have jumped at the offer. But Kahn was in his late 60s and Coven had just undergone triple bypass surgery. Stemberg wanted backers who would be tied to Staples for the long haul. Equally important, Stemberg knew that his would be a capital-intensive business. He'd probably need to return to his investors many times before the company could go public. The solution, he decided, was to raise money from institutions dedicated to backing new enterprises. So, he strode into Reilly's office one summer day and asked, "Do you guys do start-up financing?"

It was an ingenuous question. Stemberg knew that, as a rule, Downer didn't invest in new enterprises. But he also knew that Reilly ran a small portfolio of venture capital investments for a German family. Reilly listened as Stemberg expounded upon the mouth-watering business that awaited. It sounded intriguing to Reilly. They made a deal: Reilly would help raise money for Staples and, in return, Stemberg would let Reilly's German client participate in the deal.

Stemberg began toiling to exhaustively research his idea. Weeks went by. Finally he dumped a big pile of paper on Reilly's desk. Reilly plowed through some two hundred pages of spreadsheets, written analysis, and data before he pronounced judgment: "Tom, there's some interesting stuff here—but it's not a business plan." Reilly took Stemberg's materials, which he calls "a textbook exercise in researching a new business," and edited the business plan that would succeed—or fail—to persuade venture capitalists to sink millions of dollars into Stemberg's idea.

While the business plan was impressive, Stemberg knew it might not be enough to persuade investors to fork over cash. He looked at his case dispassionately and pinpointed the negatives a cautious investor might spot. Foremost among them: Stemberg himself. To his credit, he had run a billion-dollar business—experience not many entrepreneurs could claim. But he was also controversial, a bit of a wild card. He'd been fired. Some people from his past loved him, but others hated him. It was not the kind of review that inspires professional investors to open their wallets. A good business plan was not going to persuade investors that Stemberg's "wild" streak was under control. "The due diligence on Tom Stemberg could turn out to be 'He's crazy. He's nuts.' I had to deal with that issue," says Stemberg.

So he set out to make himself as acceptable as possible. His strategy: offset the negative nuances with recommendations from people whose credibility was impeccable and surround himself with directors on whom the venture capitalists felt they could rely. Here are some of his most important sponsors and how he found them:

✦ *Walter Salmon:* A thoughtful professor at Harvard Business School, Salmon taught Stemberg marketing and continued to offer career advice during Stemberg's stints at Star Markets and First National Supermarkets. "Walter is the grand old man of retailing at Harvard, even-tempered and calming. He was important in the idea formation of Staples," says Myra Hart, who is now Salmon's colleague at Harvard Business School.

✦ *Ed Cormier:* As head of operations for Edwards Supermarkets, from which Stemberg had been fired, Cormier's recommendation of Stemberg was vital.

Cormier's positive evaluation could not be made public—it could have damaged his career—but it was a powerful way to assuage potential backers' concerns.

✦ *Leo Kahn:* Stemberg converted this onetime rival at grocery chain Purity Supreme to a friend after they were guests on a local television show in 1978. He discovered that Kahn had played basketball, Stemberg's great passion, at Harvard. As president of a fund-raising organization called Friends of Harvard Basketball, Stemberg made it a point to include Kahn in banquets and other events. Ten years later, Kahn, of course, was looking for a new investment just when Stemberg was looking for a fresh career. "The role Leo played fulfilled many facets," says Myra Hart. "The money was important, but the credibility that Leo offered to Tom's investors was even more important." Adds Bob Reilly, "Kahn was tremendously successful—savvy and a good guy. People knew that if you're in a deal with him you know you're in with good people." Kahn also brought cash. Stemberg didn't want to completely fund Staples out of Kahn's bankroll, but it was comforting to know the money was there.

✦ *Don Perkins:* The former chairman of Jewel Companies, Perkins had acted as a regular source of advice and counsel for Stemberg over the years. A director of AT&T, Time, and other companies, he had strongly recommended that Stemberg start his own business.

✦ *Bob Nakasone:* Nakasone had completed the same training program at Jewel Companies that Stemberg had. By the time Stemberg began searching for a business opportunity, Nakasone was a top manager at Toys "R" Us. Smart and well-versed in every detail of superstore retailing, Nakasone helped Stemberg build the conceptual framework for Staples and served as one of Staples first board members.

✦ **Dave Lubrano:** Stemberg got to know this onetime certified public accountant, who would later become a Staples director, in 1980 when they both served on the board of Superior Brands, a small pet product maker. Lubrano was a master entrepreneur, having cofounded National Medical Care, a kidney dialysis business later sold to and spun off by W. R. Grace, and later helped establish Apollo Computer, a computer workstation company. In Stemberg he recognized a kindred soul: "He was a sharp young guy from Harvard Business School who was cutting up a big storm in the supermarket field."

Stemberg discovered Reilly, the Downer partner, through his Harvard affiliation. He discussed his plans with John McArthur, a dean of Harvard Business School, with whom he had kept in touch. McArthur sent Stemberg to Chuck Sethness, an associate dean at Harvard Business School, who suggested the would-be entrepreneur meet with the investment bankers at Downer. By the time Reilly and Stemberg had made their deal and were ready to search out investors, Stemberg had not only prepared the official selling document—the business plan—but also the unofficial sales force—his sponsors.

Real-Life Lesson

Business plans alone are not enough. *There is no end to the reassurances that folks holding the purse strings need* *before they invest in your enterprise. Any question marks about it—or you—are reason enough to back off. You must foresee any major hurdles to investment before they crop up, and devise a strategy to overcome them.* "I anticipated what the questions would be and put together an infrastructure of board members, references and managers to address those questions," says Stemberg. *The more objective you are about your greatest perceived weaknesses, the better off you will be.*

Cat and Mouse:
Playing the Venture Capital Game

All Stemberg really knew about venture capitalists when he and Reilly began searching for money in August 1985 was that he needed them. He could have scared up enough money from Leo Kahn and his friend to hot-wire Staples into existence. But he understood that he had a capital-intensive business to grow. Dozens of stores would chew up many millions of dollars. The $4 million he was now seeking was a mere drop in the bucket. If he could hook a handful of venture capitalists, he would have access to gigantic pools of capital and connections to the Wall Street firms he'd eventually need to take Staples public.

It didn't take long to learn that venture capitalists like to say no. In fact, he and Reilly found, a venture capitalist's answer is "No, No, No"—until it's "Yes." At which point they add, "I'm going to pay you as little as possible for as much of your company as I can get." Scott Meadow, a professional investor at William Blair, summed up the venture capitalist's point of view when he replied to Stemberg's pitch by saying, "Tom, you've got a great résumé. But what you're asking me to do is value your idea and your résumé for $4 million dollars, and that's just high. Ask me for a million."

To be fair, it's not as easy to be a venture capitalist as most entrepreneurs imagine. While venture capitalists do control the money, they don't truly control anything else in a company they buy into, no matter how much of it they own. They can't be certain that an entrepreneur's skills will fit those needed by the new enterprise, that his or her management team will work well together, or that the idea itself will fly. Even if they can exert control, such professional investors rarely have the operational savvy to force the business to succeed either. They can hover in the background—

> ## Bob Reilly, Partner at Downer & Co.
>
> "Coming out of food retailing, Tom was used to working on very thin margins—when you're buying something in that industry, you don't leave a fraction of a penny on the table. So he was driving the venture capital investors totally up the wall by negotiating every tiny point. I'd get a call from an investor who'd say, 'Reilly, you've got to get over here. He's driving us crazy.' My answer always was, 'You're about to invest in a company with stores aimed at producing high volume-sales at low margins. Do you want a guy who is going to roll over when he's negotiating with suppliers or someone who's going to negotiate every fraction of a penny?'"

or conspicuously in the foreground—but betting on new ventures is basically a crapshoot.

So it's easier to say "No" than "Yes"—and at first that's all Reilly and Stemberg heard. The Sprout Group in New York, a unit of Donaldson, Lufkin and Jenrette heard the duo's presentation and "politely threw us out," recalls Reilly (though they led a later round of venture financing). The money seekers got an enthusiastic hearing from one partner at Charles River Venture Partners in Boston, but the partner with veto power nixed Staples.

But there were four solid factors in Stemberg's favor. He had proven himself capable of running a big company. The business plan he and Reilly had crafted stood out for its comprehensiveness and focus on customers. Leo Kahn's support gave Stemberg's project a weight and authority that simply wouldn't have been possible for a 37-year-old to summon by himself. And, most importantly, Stemberg's idea was so powerful it practically jumped off the page.

"Frankly, what sold us was the comparison to Toys "R" Us. Staples looked like it could be a category killer," says Felda Hardymon, a partner at Bessemer Venture Partners in Wellsley Hills, Massachusetts, who had invited Downer to coinvest in another deal several years earlier.

But even Hardymon wasn't completely sold. He decided to invite Mitt Romney, a partner at Bain Capital into the picture. Boston-based Bain, a unit of Bain Consulting, was a newcomer to venture capital. After running a consulting firm for 11 years, Bill Bain, its founder, became intrigued by an idea. In order to advise their clients, Bain's consultants regularly studied industries so closely that they could spot tremendous entrepreneurial opportunities, yet they never got to dive into them. Why couldn't Bain's vast analytical talent be deployed in venture capital, where there would be a giant payoff? In 1984, Romney, one of Bain's consultants, launched Bain Capital. Hardymon thought Bain's painstaking approach would be useful in testing Stemberg's research. "Due diligence was a real thing with them. You could ask a rhetorical question and some Bain consultant would go out, do research for two days, and come back with answers," he explains.

Indeed, Bain investigated every nook and cranny of Stemberg's premise. "At first I thought it was a crazy idea," recalls Romney. "Business services were moving toward becoming more convenient, but this idea involved asking businesses to do their own shopping." He decided to study the idea more closely. A team of four consultants called forty companies to ask how much they spent on office supplies. Glumly, they reported the answer to Stemberg: only $200 per employee. "I said, 'Look guys, I agree that it's not a top-of-mind problem. Do me a favor and audit the invoices.' And because they were new, they were rookies, the Bain consultants actually did it," says Stemberg. The new answer:

$800 per person. The money that customers could save was, in the end, what persuaded Romney. "There were some big risks, but we knew that if people behaved as rational economic beings they'd come shop at Staples," Romney says.

Stemberg reeled in Fred Adler, a New York lawyer who dabbled in venture capital, after meeting one of his junior partners, Sandy Samuels, through a headhunter friend. Samuels liked Stemberg's presentation immediately. Hambro, a New York venture firm approached by Reilly, also sensed a good opportunity.

By November of 1985, Bessemer, Bain, Adler, and Hambro had finished sniffing the deal and wanted in. But in the odd world of venture capital, nobody wanted to make the first move. Explains Reilly: "Venture capitalists have a well-developed herd instinct. If one buffalo starts to run, all the buffalos will run. But if no buffalo starts, no one will run." The bison that moved: Adler, who was not a card-carrying member of the venture capital industry and thus had no compunction about breaking ranks with the other venture capitalists by saying "Yes." Bain, Bessemer and Hambro fell into line quickly. They didn't want to lose the deal, and "they hated to see Adler get it," says Stemberg.

Negotiations, nonetheless, dragged on over price. The central tension in any venture capital deal: how much the yet-to-be-established company is worth. A company's "valuation," as it is known, governs how much money an entrepreneur raises as well as how much of the company the entrepreneur will own. Venture capitalists yearn to keep the valuation low. Entrepreneurs want to push the number up. In this case, Stemberg thought Staples was worth $8 million. He wanted to raise $4 million for 50 percent of the company. The venture capitalists wanted to value the company at $6 million—which would have netted Stemberg and his team only $2 million.

As Bessemer's Hardymon and Stemberg wrestled with the valuation issue, the entrepreneur grew demoralized. Staples didn't have a shot at success if it was not adequately funded. And to get the $4 million it needed, the venture capitalists were demanding between 70 and 80 percent ownership of the company. If venture capitalists were controlling the company, would he have the decision-making power necessary to make it succeed?

Stemberg poured out his concerns to Dave Lubrano over Czech beer in a Prague bar. They had flown to Eastern Europe for a Superior Brands board meeting. Lubrano, a veteran well-acquainted with venture capitalists, gave Stemberg a much-needed shot of entrepreneurial boosterism. Lubrano said, "Hey, you can't trust these guys. The venture community is just out to cut the best deal they can for themselves and their partners." Lubrano emphasized how terrific the Staples idea was and encouraged Stemberg to stick to his guns. If the venture capitalists were going to be so greedy, he said, "Tell them to go screw themselves."

Thus fortified, Stemberg flew back to Boston and insisted upon a better deal. Was he scared that he would end up without backers? "No," says Stemberg. "The venture capitalists operate as a cartel. I only figured it out later

TOM STEMBERG

"The venture capitalists tried price fixing on me. When they said that the valuation of Staples was just too rich for them, I'd say: 'I'd really like to have you as an investor. The stock is going to be sold for this price. I hope you're not upset when I don't come back to you later (in future financing rounds), because I'd like to. But I just want a fair price for the stock and I'm going to get it.'"

on. They talk to each other and they agree on the valuation they want. I broke the cartel by getting people outside the club, like Adler—who would have been willing to invest without the others—and Bain, which was new and not really part of the club." On January 23, 1986, he struck a deal: The venture capitalists would pay $4.5 million for 56 percent of the company. Staples was worth $8 million.

Real-Life Lesson

No one will ever value your business as highly as you do. *That's the way it should be. No one can see a new enterprise's potential—and the steps needed to fulfill it—as clearly as the person who is risking his livelihood on the idea. That means you will face skepticism at every turn, particularly from potential investors. But remember: a company's valuation is as much a test of conviction as a true measure of potential. No one really knows how a new business will fare.*

Round Two: Breaking the Venture Capitalist Cartel

Stemberg entered the ring swinging in round two. This time he had a lot more leverage: his idea was working in spades. He had opened one highly successful store with the first round of capital and their prospects were bright. Sales per square foot at Staples stores were increasing rapidly. The first Brighton store had opened with a forecast of $4 million in annual sales, but it was quickly zooming toward $6 million a year. "We kept beating our forecasts. The results were exciting enough to cause a lot of people to sit up and take notice," recalls Bob Leombruno, who reported monthly results to the venture capitalists. But Staples would need to expand quickly. Within five months of the Brighton store's opening, a clone called Office Depot began opening stores in the southeast. Staples needed more money to stake out its territory—fast.

But the venture capitalists entered round two with their gloves up, too. "Now they said, 'You know he nailed us the first round. Let's go get it back,'" says Stemberg. They urged Stemberg to take a backseat in raising capital so he wouldn't be distracted from running the company. They offered to bring in a blue-ribbon panel of investors such as J. H. Whitney and Rockefeller in New York. And they had already marked up a price tag for Staples: $15 million. Venture capitalists had a rule of thumb, they reasoned: In a second-round financing, they never value a company at more than twice its first-round valuation.

Stemberg was determined to do better. Venture capitalists had pegged Home Club, a home improvement retailer similar to Home Depot, at $22 million in a recent financing. What's more, he knew that there had to be other investors willing to pay up to participate in the Staples story.

Bob Leombruno,
Former Chief Financial Officer

"We turned money away in the first and second rounds. There was a second company called Office Depot that opened about nine months after our first round. They were run by very experienced retail people from Grossman's Lumber and functioned similarly to Staples. They were jumping all over the southeast. Immediately all of the venture capitalists who funded retail start-ups understood the potential of these stores. You didn't have to be a rocket scientist. We were seeing sales figures of $300 to $800 per square foot. High-volume discounters were lucky to do $300 per square foot."

So Stemberg decided to give his venture capitalists a little competition. He asked Goldman Sachs, a New York investment firm, to prepare a capital-raising proposal. Goldman's proposal landed on Stemberg's desk two weeks later. What did the firm say Staples was worth? $15 million—exactly the venture capitalists' number. Pressing the investment bankers, Stemberg learned that Goldman thought it could raise more for Staples, but had plugged in the rule-of-thumb figure after consulting with the venture capital community. Exasperated, Stemberg said, "If you want to value the company at the same level as the venture capitalists, I don't need you. If you want to raise the amount it's worth, we can go ahead." The next day he got a call from Goldman. Tear the valuation page out of the proposal, the bankers directed Stemberg, we've got a new one: The firm said it could value Staples at $22 million!

With the Goldman proposal in hand, Stemberg decided to call his venture capitalists' bluff. After they were all assembled around a table at the next board meeting, he told them that he had received a better offer. He said he'd be willing to cut them in on the deal at a slight discount, but that he was prepared to hire Goldman if they could not match the valuation. Bessemer dug in its heels at $15 million. Hambro waffled. Mitt Romney split ranks by saying that he didn't know what Bain Capital was willing to do, but that several of his limited partners were willing to put up their own money at Stemberg's price.

The following week, while the first-round venture capitalists struggled to come to an agreement, Stemberg found two investors who had no qualms about how he valued Staples. Marty Trust, the head of Mast Industries, whose office in Woburn, Massachusetts, was across the street from Staples' second store, wanted to buy 10 percent of Staples. "Well, that will be $3 million," said Stemberg. "Fine," said Trust. Ricardo Poma, a limited partner of Bain Capital, invested $750,000, at the same valuation.

Excerpt from Geyer's Office Dealer (July 1987)

"If a few attractive stores with somewhat limited merchandise could conquer the world, there'd be a Drawing Board [stationery store] on every corner. . . . As of today, no would-be national network has been able to surmount the obstacles to profitable growth, though there's no end to trying . . . The Staples Inc. directorate includes top executives of Toys "R" Us and a home improvement chain. We fail to see any synergy here. Barry Frahm, president of O Henry, a regional wholesaler and also of the Wholesale Stationers Association, said recently that price clubs, though feared by dealers, are really not that threatening. Few offer service and when they do, they'll have to charge for it."

When Stemberg then returned to his first-round backers, he had alarming news. It began to look like they might be crowded out. "This thing's filling up fast. Do you guys want to play or not?" It worked. The venture capitalist group, which included Citicorp, Blair Ventures, and Security Pacific, agreed on the $22 million figure.

Real-Life Lesson

The more deep pockets you locate, the better your negotiating position. *Different investors will value your business differently. Marty Trust's retailing background made him put more of a premium on Staples' high sales-per-square-foot than the venture capitalists. Stemberg also discovered that there were plenty of other institutional investors who would be happy to accord Staples a higher valuation. Without their differing perspectives, Stemberg might have ended up with significantly less money to build the business and a smaller ownership position.*

4 | OF LANDLORDS AND REAL ESTATE

Instant success bequeathed Staples with instant inadequacy. One successful store was not enough to make its imprint felt throughout Boston. Three Boston stores were not enough to hold off competitors from coming into the northeast. A dozen northeastern stores wouldn't stake out Staples' turf across the rest of the country. Finding and securing the right real estate is a deadly serious concern for any retailer. For Staples it was even more so. "When you're the CEO, driving around looking at real estate is the most important thing you can do," explains Stemberg. "If you're in the retail business, it's everything. We couldn't afford to advertise much. Your biggest advertisement is the storefront itself. Everything rests on your ability to create a monument out there on a Route 9 or a Route 1."

The most serious roadblock to leasing stores was Staples' short track record. The last thing a landlord wants to do is make a bet on an unproven business. What's more, any real estate owner who was interested enough to make inquiries about this revolutionary kind of store would not have been encouraged; the scuttlebutt buzzing through office supply and stationery circles was that Staples would never make it. "When you're just starting and no one knows anything about your business, they're fearful of leasing to you and won't make any improvements to the building. The weaker your balance sheet, the higher the rent," says Steve Westerfield, former CEO of WORKplace, a competitor that Staples acquired in 1991.

Today most folks know Staples superstores as huge spaces between 17,000 and 24,000 square feet with a red-and-white pylon sign outside. But to land a site when it was still a young company, Staples was forced into being flexible. The company converted restaurants and massage parlors into Staples stores and even fashioned one California building into a flying saucer shape to satisfy Los Angeles building officials.

"Most of our jobs were frantic. In many places we ran into asbestos. We had contractors abandon jobs. One of our contractors in Portchester, New York, was literally working day and night. I'll never forget going to the store and finding his bed—he was living there until the job was done," remembers Myra Hart. Ron Sargent, vice president of operations in 1989, remembers one of the company's real estate representatives describing her tour of a prospective Staples store: "She was walking through the building and happened to look down at the floor. I guess there was some sort of toxic waste on the floor and her shoes were starting to melt."

Flexibility also meant learning how to live with even the most idiosyncratic landlords. Joe Vassalluzzo, executive vice president of global growth and development at Staples, had followed the fortunes of one eccentric Delaware landlord-developer for years. The developer owned a former elementary school in Wilmington that he planned to turn into a shopping center. But there were a myriad of environmental and zoning hurdles to clear before he could begin construction. The obstacles were so daunting that many observers believed he'd never get the necessary approvals. But the developer steadfastly held onto the property and, finally, after a decade of ownership, he was able to construct a shopping center.

Joe Vassalluzzo

"Most real estate developers who lease to us are local. In 25 to 30 percent of the cases, the property we're negotiating over is the only one they own. They're a very eclectic group, but there's a common theme. They're self-made—very driven, very assertive and aggressive. They're going to be adversarial. Their sense of loyalty is distorted from the usual sense of the word. I'll never forget shaking hands with a national developer at a conference I was attending. He was telling me how much he loves Staples and what a great company it is. We're standing at his company's booth and I look up to see we're shaking hands underneath a gigantic blown-up photograph of an Office Depot store he owned—our main competitor."

Vassalluzzo began to negotiate for a site, but the potential transaction seemed doomed. The landlord wanted an outrageously high rent—some 30 percent higher than the going rate—but the location was exceptional. He also insisted that Staples conform to his center's color scheme: brick with green signage and trim. "Even though we were anxious to secure the site, we told him the rent was highway robbery," recalls Vassalluzzo. The landlord retorted that he'd find a competitor, but Vassalluzzo and his team thought it was a bluff. Nothing happened for several months. Then out of the blue, the developer called Vassalluzzo and began talking to him in a whisper. Vassalluzzo could barely hear him, so he asked the developer why he was whispering.

"Because I'm at the other guy's place," the developer answered in a barely audible voice. It turned out that Intelligent Electronics, a Wilmington company, was contemplating opening a superstore and was interested in the new store site. But the developer preferred Staples as a tenant and was calling to give him one last chance to take the site. Knowing the landlord's eccentricities, Vassalluzzo believed him and decided that he was willing to pay the outrageous rent if the landlord would sign Staples' standard lease. "I'll sign anything," the landlord promised. "As long as the rent is right."

One of Staples' midwestern stores was built in the parking lot of a furniture store owned by a local couple. Though the couple clearly enjoyed getting Staples' rent check every month, they weren't especially pleased about all of the characteristics that went along with a retail superstore. Armed with binoculars, they watched the parking lot like hawks for misdemeanors—shopping carts left in the lot, employees parking in the wrong spots, sloppy trash collectors—and called promptly to complain. "You name it—it was an issue," recalls Vassalluzzo. "Our general manager was pulling his hair out."

Periodically the couple would become so agitated that they would summon Vassalluzzo and Sargent to a summit meeting. During one visit, Vassalluzzo walked through the large, empty furniture store searching for the couple. "It was full of totally bizarre furniture. I was getting the sensation of being on the set of Sunset Boulevard. In came the woman looking like Gloria Swanson with a five-foot beehive, black toreador slacks, and heels," remembers Vassalluzzo.

The tirade began. She knew all of the Staples' employees by name and itemized their sins. One had thrown a wrapper on the ground in the parking lot during his lunch break. Another employee had parked in a space reserved for the furniture store's nonexistent customers. Finally, admonished the woman, "And that one girl, Debby, somebody should tell her that she wears her bra too loose." Vassalluzzo looked at Sargent. Sargent looked at Vassalluzzo. "It was like the Twilight Zone," says Sargent.

Why bother with such eccentrics? Staples needed the store site, of course. But it also operates with a credo that would serve any business: your landlord is your business partner. "Recognize that a landlord is making a huge investment in you," urges Stemberg. "If you sign a lease for 20,000 square feet at $20 a square foot, that's $400,000 a year. If you sign a ten-year lease, that's a $4 million commitment that guy made to you. He's betting that you're going to stay in business. If you go broke, it's going to take him two or three years to get his real estate back through the court system."

Real-Life Lesson

Your landlord is one of the biggest investors in your business. *Everything about the landlord-tenant relationship conspires to make you adversaries. You want a low rent rate. Your landlord wants it high. You want the space improved. Your landlord doesn't want to spend a nickel on it. It's the natural state of affairs. Just don't forget that your landlord is making a significant contribution to your company.* "Landlords are backers, as are venture capitalists," asserts Stemberg. "You need to treat them the right way even though they can be animals and it's hard to treat them the right way."

The Agony and The Ecstasy

Staples' hunger for real estate grew intense in 1989. Between 1986, when it was founded, and 1989, the company opened twenty-five stores. But in 1989, the competition was multiplying and Staples, having gone public, finally had the capital to expand massively. And it did. From 1989 to 1995, it opened a store every eight days—or nearly one a week. To pull off this astonishing feat, Staples had to pour resources into acquiring stores. The first step had been hiring Vassalluzzo, president of American Stores Properties Inc., a subsidiary of American Stores Co. Vassalluzzo's mission: To build a real estate machine that could support Staples' hypergrowth. The company's real estate staff grew from one manager and one researcher to nearly fifteen executives who would comb the country searching for location, location, location. More important, Staples' real estate unit has developed a sophisticated software model to analyze store sites. "Today, if you give me an intersection, we can tell you the population count, small business count, and prospective store volume," says Henry Flieck, vice president of real estate.

But one key factor drove Staples' real estate quest: boundless energy in the face of uncertainty and endless obstacles. It is not hard to actually find a good store location. They are there to be seen and inspected. Good research can readily tell Staples whether the place has a high density of small businesses nearby. The hard part is negotiating for a store, which can take from three months to a year. "You never have control during that time period," explains Vassalluzzo. "Yet you're planning the store and acting like you have control. Then after ten months of negotiation when you're finally set for a signature, out of nowhere a competitor comes in and says, 'I'll pay whatever to take that lease away.' You live in a constant state of fear and terror."

The "what ifs" add immensely to the uncertainty. A typical contract lease will consist of a firm ten-year commitment and a series of renewals, which usually adds twenty more years. The time span alone opens up a multitude of possibilities: what if the state puts in a superhighway in the year 2010; what if all the other stores in the strip mall close; who is responsible for the myriad ways the store can be damaged? Staples, like any retail store, has to make extensive promises about how often it will be open and how long it will be open.

There is plenty to argue over. So, reaching an agreement with a landlord not only takes time, it takes thick

RON SARGENT, PRESIDENT, STAPLES CONTRACT AND COMMERCIAL

"Today there's a lot of quantitative modeling about where to place a store, but in the beginning we did things differently. We located stores in areas that were high density for businesses, but were not historically good retail locations. Now we look for the density of business but also for good retail locations because a good chunk of our customers are consumers. Early on, we wanted stores to be a ten-minute drive away, but now that we've recognized that small towns are good markets for us, some stores are an hour-long drive. I remember having this conversation with Tom [Stemberg] about putting a store in Dayton, Ohio. Staples was in Columbus and Cincinnati, and Dayton was right in the middle. But Dayton was a big company town with a few hundred thousand people and Tom's conclusion was: It's too small to support a superstore. Now there are four superstores in Dayton—all of them doing very well—but unfortunately none of them are Staples stores."

skin. According to Vassalluzzo, "The best way to describe the approach of most landlord-developers is that when you first make contact, they immediately strike you over the head with a two-by-four as hard as they can. If you survive the blow, you're worthy of negotiating with them."

In California, however, landlords use a different but equally painful approach. "They kind of befriend you. Instead of using a two-by-four, they use a 'one-by-three' and hit you softly about a thousand times," he says. The best example was Robert, a Los Angeles developer in his late forties, who drove a Jaguar with a license plate that read "DECLAWED." Robert had remarried for the third time, he explained to Vassalluzzo. Finding the true love of his life had removed his claws. But the process seemed to have also removed his ability to make quick decisions. Guided by his accountant and a financial advisor who was also his spiritual advisor, it took six months before he could even decide to begin negotiating with Staples. "I guess he was trying to become one with the universe," says Vassalluzzo. Finally, after two years of negotiation, Staples and Robert were able to conclude the transaction.

Hard, cold cash holds sway even in the most orderly of settings. At one bankruptcy auction, Vassalluzzo had his eye on a Framingham, Massachusetts, location in which he felt few retailers would be interested. Bankruptcy auctions, which are legal proceedings, many times turn into circus sideshows. The representatives, or agents, hired by the court are expert at generating the maximum amount of money for the bankrupt estate and have little interest in anything else. At one particular auction, a former toy superstore was available for the apparent bargain price of $350,000, with little or no prior interest in the location from other retailers. Much to Vassalluzzo's and everyone else's surprise, a bevy of retailers showed up at the court and serious bidding commenced among the group. It was fast and furious, and the asking price quickly escalated to the range of $1.5 million, to the delight of the court and the representatives. Near the bidding's conclusion, the trustee summarized the bids with obvious intent of keeping his eye on the money and not much on anything else. As he attempted to summarize who bid what new retailing names emerged. For example, MVP Sports became "the sporting goods outfit." Computer City became "the computer guys from Dallas." And Fretters, a consumer electronics retailer, became "Fritters." He may have had difficulty with their names, but not the amounts they bid.

Real-Life Lesson

In retail real estate, you spend your life trying to control things over which you have no control. *The only way to deal with the uncertainty is to forge ahead, building your company's plans around the belief that the store will actually open while also pursuing alternative sites. In August of 1995, for example, Staples' marketing, merchandising, and information systems were designing their operational plans on the assumption that Staples would open more than one hundred stores in 1996, though only 35 percent of the leases had been executed. Vassalluzzo concludes, "A deal is not a deal until it is signed, no matter how many conditional letters of contract you've signed, no matter how many hands you've shaken."*

Stealing Home Base: Defensive Real Estate

The beauty of nailing down a prime store location is that in one fell swoop you establish your presence while preempting your competitors. Because the market for office supply superstores is far from saturated, securing real estate continues to be as much a key competitive strategy as it is fuel for Staples' growth. "It's a race," explains Vassalluzzo. "Real estate is like diamonds—scarce and irreplaceable. Once you have it, the chance of a competitor finding something comparable is slim. There's an ending to the story. Eventually there will be a saturation point. The total number of superstores that North America will support? Probably twenty-eight hundred retail stores or more. By the end of this year there will be about fourteen hundred stores."

Gem properties stimulate as much intrigue as a Tom Clancy best-seller. Scuttlebutt about store sites circulates constantly among brokers, agents, store representatives, and merchants. It is no secret that a choice spot will be coming on the market. The secret is how to get it—or keep it away from your competitors. In one of its biggest victories in the turf war, Staples had been trying to snare three Baltimore stores that had belonged to Office Stop, a competitor that had gone bankrupt. The bankruptcy court, in San Antonio, Texas, was demanding stringent terms, though, so Staples halted negotiations.

But Office Depot, Staples' biggest competitor, wanted the same stores. Just before the court was due to award the property in a sealed bid auction, Vassalluzzo learned that Office Depot had negotiated a deal with Office Stop, subject to the court's approval. So he decided to make a dramatic, last-minute bid for the stores. He flew all night and, over Office Depot's loud objections, presented himself in front of the judge the next morning with a suitcase full of cash. "The judge was a riverboat gambler," says Vassalluzzo. "He said, they're here, they're real and they have a bag full of money. They can participate in the auction." Within hours, Staples was declared the winner. It was an excellent offensive play. It prevented Office Depot from blocking Staples and at the same time enabled Staples to enter the Baltimore market with several stores at once.

The keep-away game gets tough when Staples senses intruders in markets where it has a major presence. In 1992, it got wind that OfficeMax hoped to enter the Boston metropolitan market by buying six stores from Highland Superstores, a failed electronics and appliance chain. Stemberg and Vassalluzzo were determined not to let it happen. They flew through a snowstorm to Detroit, where the chain was based, and met with Highland's chairman and head of real estate operations at 10:00 P.M. The past few days at Highland's offices had been quite heady as one CEO after another had visited in an effort to snag the stores. "Every day there's someone else," said the real estate

Henry Flieck, Vice President of Real Estate

"When I joined Staples in 1990, everything was relatively manual in terms of site investigation. We used to literally take population counts by zip code. We worked out a somewhat analytical and somewhat seat-of-the-pants estimate of a prospective store's sales volume. We worked a lot of weekends and nights to get the math figured. Today if you draw a twelve-mile ring around a prospective store site, our computer will automatically diminish the volumes and population figures as you get further away from the store. We used to do that manually."

executive. "What we have here is a very hot property."

As the meeting progressed, though, Stemberg and Vassalluzzo learned that Highland's properties weren't what they originally thought. First, Highland insisted on selling the stores in a package. Staples did not want all of them. Second, and more important, the chain needed landlord consent to transfer the properties. They could not sublet the stores unless the landlord approved the new tenant. Stemberg and Vassalluzzo walked out of that meeting happy as clams. "Rather than trying to negotiate with these guys, we decided we're just going to go after the stores we want—through the *landlords,* not through Highland." They visited the owners of Highland's Brighton, Weymouth, and Danvers stores and cut deals with them. If and when the owners got the sites back, Staples would capture them.

In the meantime, OfficeMax prematurely announced its pending triumph: It was coming to Boston with a six-store package purchased from Highland. A flurry of fearful analyst reports flew out of Wall Street. Stemberg recalls, "They said this would have a devastating impact on Staples—we couldn't survive the first real competition we'd ever had in our home territory. Blah, blah, blah." OfficeMax didn't have long to gloat. When it tried to actually execute new leases on the three stores that Staples wanted, it confronted landlords who simply said, "Sorry. We want the store back."

"That kind of trench warfare was very instrumental. OfficeMax ended up with a really lousy package of stores—one of which they've already closed—and paid big money for it, too. And we extracted the crown jewels from the package," summarizes Stemberg. Once again, the strategy paid double dividends. It expanded Staples territory while preventing a competitor from getting good locations. But it required some fancy footwork. Staples was able to simply convert one of the Highland stores. But the Weymouth, Massachusetts, space was adjacent to a shopping center where Staples already had a store. So the company moved its store into the Highland space and sublet the old space to a store that sold auto parts. Staples later decided it did not want the third location, so that was sublet to a computer superstore. "These are very high-risk transactions," says Vassalluzzo.

Real-Life Lesson

The best defense is a good offense. *Figure out what's the central scarce resource in your business and scrap for it. At Staples, good real estate drives sales growth, protects you from competitors, and, sometimes, can be a weapon against enemies. In your business, the resource might be information or craftsmanship. Find it, fight for it, and don't let your competitors get their hands on it.*

5 COMPETITION: FRIEND AND FOE

Within weeks after it opened its first store in 1986, Staples was making waves. Joe Antonini, chairman of Kmart, walked through the doors. And the word was that Wal-Mart executives had visited too. Charles Lazarus, the chairman of Toys "R" Us who was also on Wal-Mart's board, attended a Wal-Mart board meeting at which Staples was described as the best, new retail concept of the year. He passed the compliment on to Bob Nakasone, one of his managers and a Staples director. In the hypercompetitive field of retailing, any new experiment is worth checking out. It wasn't surprising that the retailing giants had come to inspect the store—the shock was that they had shown up so quickly!

The speed at which news of Staples had burst upon the retailing world would be a decisive factor in its success. If Stemberg's idea worked, Staples could expect other entrepreneurs and retailers to clone its store—but not for a year or so. Serious competition might not spring up until Staples went public, when its financials would be available for public consumption. That delay would grant Staples a giant head start, time in which to blanket key regions of the country with Staples stores. Being first might give Staples a chance to dominate the industry for decades.

But this time it didn't work that way. The first imitator began ringing up sales five months after shopping carts had begun rolling through Staples' Brighton store. Within

Tom Stemberg

> "Probably the one thing we did wrong, we did by accident because we lived here. It's much tougher to do business in the Northeast than in the Sun Belt. It was a huge advantage for Office Depot that they started out without the obstacles of dealing with New York authorities and expensive media. Everything was cheaper down in Florida."

two short years Staples, amazingly, had twenty competitors. But the proliferation did not occur because giants such as Home Depot and Wal-Mart charged after Staples. The force fueling the explosion of copycats was actually the venture capital community. Flush with cash from previous deals that had successfully gone public, venture capitalists were especially receptive to new retailing concepts. And to add fuel to the fire, two of Staples closest advisors helped put Staples most powerful competitor—Office Depot—on the map.

Stemberg had asked Mike Grossman, founder of Grossman's Lumber based in Braintree, Massachusetts, to serve on Staples' board because his experience operating a chain of home improvement stores would lend Staples expertise and credibility with venture capitalists. Not long after Grossman agreed, Pat Sher, an acquaintance, asked him if he would act as a character reference. An entrepreneur who had cofounded Mr. How, a failed Home Depot clone, Sher was casting about for a new venture. Grossman agreed to be a reference. His support made Sher's enterprise—which turned out to be Office Depot—"financeable."

Another Staples backer, Fred Adler, actually helped fill Office Depot's coffers. Just about the time Staples' first store opened, Sher asked Adler to invest in Office Depot.

Adler demurred, saying that he had a conflict of interest because he was a Staples investor. But he offered to refer the opportunity to another venture capitalist. Instead of calling an independent firm, the usual practice, he passed the deal on to Joe Pagano, an investment advisor from Aspen, Colorado. Pagano, however, was not a wholly independent third party. He managed the trusts of Adler's children.

Once they got wind of Adler's move, Staples' other backers were angry. Bain's Romney and Bessemer's Hardymon flew to New York to confront Adler in his Park Avenue law offices. Adler, an aggressive corporate attorney legendary for his temper, was insulted and indignant. "Look," Adler protested. "There is not conflict of interest. It's only my children who are doing the investing in Office Depot." When Romney and Hardymon chided Adler over this excuse, he retorted, "It's none of your business. If you have a problem with it, talk to Tom."

As Stemberg prepared to meet with Adler, he got a cautionary call from one of Adler's partners. "He said, 'Fred's about to explode over this. The secretaries are diving for cover,'" remembers Stemberg. Sure enough, when Stemberg walked into Adler's office, he found a volcano primed to erupt. Adler was sitting in his customary spot, a leather desk chair that elevated him several inches higher than anyone else seated in his office. As Stemberg sat gazing up at him, Adler let it loose. There was no conflict of interest, he insisted. *He* wasn't investing in Office Depot. Besides, he didn't like taking orders. Bain was an unseasoned venture capital firm. "What the hell is a snotpicker like Romney telling me what to do?" he screamed. As for Hardymon, continued the lawyer, he'd been hanging around with uptight Yankees too long. He just would not be treated this way, Adler insisted. "You mess with me and you know what? I'm going to crush you!" he angrily concluded, pulling a legal pad off of his desk and crushing it between his hands.

Having a well-financed competitor was worrisome, but what was especially disheartening was that Office Depot had it so easy. Where Staples had had to laboriously invent itself from scratch, Office Depot breezed into the business by copying everything the Boston company did. Krasnow explains, "They didn't have to do any research. Their early positioning was simply to go to vendors and say, 'Whatever you're selling to Staples, sell to us.' So they got started in half the time that it took us."

The Florida start-up was such an unabashed imitator that it even copied Staples' mistakes. One of Staples' first marketing brochures, for example, contained a typo. Shopping at Staples, it declared, was "hassel-free." When it had its own marketing literature printed up, Office Depot didn't even

---

Bo Cheadle, Securities Analyst at Montgomery Securities

"Staples pursued a fortress strategy. It determined that if it were successful, it would attract a lot of competitors. So it entered into high-cost markets and built relatively small stores—to lessen the need for capital and lower operating costs. However, what Staples didn't factor in was that the money would flow into the business so rapidly that the cycle would be compressed. A cycle that would normally have taken ten years was squeezed into two or three years. What caused that change was technology and the venture capitalists' huge appetite for new retail concepts. So everybody got into the business. Then it obviously became much more difficult."

---

bother to correct the spelling. Shopping at Office Depot, its hot-off-the-presses brochure boasted, was "hassel-free," too.

As Staples and Office Depot began to demonstrate that selling office supplies in a superstore was tremendously profitable, venture capitalists began to scramble over each other to get a piece of the future fortune. "You could see that Staples was clearly going to be a success and there was an enormous market out there. Those venture capitalists who didn't participate in Staples or Office Depot started throwing money at other clones," says Bo Cheadle, a securities analyst at Montgomery Securities. By the end of 1988, Office Depot had twenty-six stores to Staples' twenty-two. Office Club had opened fifteen, BizMart had established ten, and OfficeMax had launched fewer than a dozen. More than a dozen other clones, including WORKplace, HQ Office Supplies Warehouse, HQ International, Office World and Office Place, each had two to seven stores in place. Small surprise, then, that when Stemberg was asked in 1989 how it felt to be the father of the office supplies superstore industry, he replied: "I wish I had worn a condom."

TODD KRASNOW

"By building these networks [of stores] in these big markets like New York and Boston, we have kept competitors out for a very, very long period of time. Office Depot only came to metro New York in late 1995. They're not in New York with any meaningful presence, they're not in Boston, and they're not in Philadelphia or anywhere in between. One of the reasons is we have a very, very good network and it's really tough to steal the customer from a direct competitor when you don't have the economies of advertising leverage."

Real-Life Lesson

You can't keep the competition away from a good idea. *Few businesses make copycatting as easy as retailing. But any superior business concept—or improvement upon a concept—will draw better-financed, more powerful competitors. "Confidentiality agreements mean nothing," says Stemberg. If you're successful, you can't prevent others from trying to enter your domain. But you can focus your energies on executing your idea better than anyone else.*

The Upside: Cherry-Picking Competitors' Best Ideas

Though they were imitating Stemberg's basic retail idea, the Staples clones were not identical to one another. Staples was trying to build a critical mass of stores in the northeast to shut out competitors and make it cost-effective to advertise in the region's high-cost media. Office Depot, in Florida, had larger stores than Staples' and plenty of money to advertise heavily and expand quickly. Office Club, which was run by Mark Begelman, a former furniture retailing executive, fashioned itself after Price Club, the grocery wholesale chain. Launched in California, it charged customers to become members, carried fewer items, but offered prices even lower than Staples'.

While the differences were troubling—because they forced Staples executives to reexamine their own strategy—they were also exciting. For the first time, Staples could scrutinize other retailers' ideas—and filch the best ones. "Some of the chains were ahead of their time in being very consumer-friendly. In 1988, the home market wasn't what it is today. These chains didn't have the bread-and-butter business customer, but they came up with interesting ways to display product and design their stores," says Krasnow.

As Staples executives knew, gathering intelligence on the competition could be as simple as visiting a store. But at first, Staples' own view of the world prevented it from appreciating alternative approaches. In 1987, Stemberg sent two managers down to Florida to study Office Depot's first four stores. Posing as customers, they walked through every aisle, studied Office Depot employees, estimated the number of items being sold, and compared prices. Their first, overwhelming impression: The stores were a mess. Packaging littered the floor, boxes of goods had been ripped open,

Excerpt from a Memo Assessing Office Depot's Stores

"They make very little effort in the areas of customer service. We asked a number of questions of various employees at [sic] which we received fair to poor responses. They appeared indifferent and basically uninformed. In the area of service to the consumer, it simply came down to our having Consultants, Management and employees in general trained and available to assist the customer where Office Depot had a work force designed to strickly [sic] deal with product packout and display. . . . [Stock] maintenance was quite poor in all locations. Many out of stocks, shelves not straightened and shelf tags that were missing, outdated and in wrong locations. . . . We personally felt much better about our operation and were not impressed by their lack of standards and personnel. If we were to put a store up against them there's no doubt we would be much superior."

This memo is a perfect example of how easily you can be blinded by your own self-confidence. Stemberg says, "When you go to somebody else's store, the last thing you want to discuss is how the competitor is screwing up. You want to find out what those guys do better than you."

---

merchandise tickets were missing, and store shelves had big empty spaces where items had been sold out. The duo did not find it hard to reach a conclusion. "They said Office Depot was never going to make it," remembers Krasnow.

In fact, Office Depot not only "made it," the Florida clone outstripped Staples, becoming the largest office supplies retailer in the country, with an estimated $5.5 billion in 1995 sales. So what happened? "In hindsight, what the ripped boxes and messy stores reflected was that their prices were really, really good," explains Krasnow. "Customers were snapping up merchandise. Office Depot had challenges that needed to be overcome, but the basic demand was there. And they obviously became very, very successful."

Not long afterwards, Staples' managers got a lesson in how willing competitors were to take espionage activities to an extreme. In 1988, the company was preparing to open its Springfield, Virginia, store. The store was located in a mall in which Montgomery Ward was an anchor. The mall was open, but Staples was still under construction. A wall divided Staples' store from Montgomery Ward, which happened to own a stake in Office World, one of Staples' competitors. Staples' managers had no reason to give Montgomery Ward's relationship to Office World a second thought until several days before the Springfield grand opening. As managers and associates were busily setting up merchandise inside the new space, they were startled to see a stranger filming the inside of the store with a video camera. Obviously the man had climbed the dividing wall to gain entry. Several Staples associates quickly extracted the tape from the camera and escorted the man out of the mall.

The message was clear: spy or be spied upon. Staples executives lost no time in poring over other chains' techniques and innovations. "I used to shop with my mother-in-law," remembers Stemberg. She had an apartment in Ft. Lauderdale and together they put the nearest Office Depot store through its paces. She'd order paper clips, pens, and paper to be delivered to her apartment, then call to complain and ask that the stuff be picked up and returned to the store. "I really wanted to understand how they did everything, what their systems were like, what they had in stock, and what they couldn't do," says Stemberg. "I visited stores constantly—it's not like they'd ever recognize me."

On another occasion, he had his wife, Dola, apply for a job at Office Depot's Atlanta delivery-order center. She said she had experience in telemarketing and, in a soft, southern accent, explained to the interviewer that she was anxious to move back "home." Staples did not offer delivery service at the time, so Stemberg wanted to investigate how Office Depot's delivery system worked, how many people were in the operation, and how it trained employees. Dola stopped the application process before the company even offered her a job interview, but Stemberg still got the information.

Some of Staples' sleuthing seemed more like a scene from Laurel and Hardy than James Bond. During a visit to competitive stores in Florida, five executives, including Krasnow, visited Office Depot's North Miami Beach store. While scouring the facility for information, Krasnow noticed the employee schedule posted on a bulletin board and quickly made a mental note of all the pertinent numbers. Fifteen minutes later, the Staples executives were preparing to leave the Office Depot store when all of the sudden they heard a commotion. One of the Staples executives was racing down an aisle, waving a piece of paper in his hand and crying, "I got the schedule! I got the schedule!" Behind him, a half-dozen Office Depot associates were in hot pursuit. "It was the same report that I saw," says Krasnow. "We all bolted out of the store and ran to the parking lot."

Real-Life Lesson

Never underestimate your competitors. *It's all too easy to believe that your strategy is superior to a competitor's. You've chosen it because you believe in it. But underestimating your competitors can only hurt you. Even the worst of them probably has one or two ideas from which you could benefit. And you can be sure they're poring over your approach, too. Scrapping for competitive information is vital when you're small.*

Changing Alliances: Redrawing The Battlefield

"Retail is detail," Stemberg often said in Staples' early days. But as the superstore chains began to grow, Staples' need for market intelligence shifted. Now it needed to learn about its competitors' plans as well as store operations. In 1989, Staples heard that Office Warehouse would be entering the Philadelphia marketplace. Stemberg and Vassalluzzo were traveling around the region with a broker, wondering where the sites were—and if they were any good. The next day the broker obligingly reported where Office Warehouse planned to locate its stores. "How do you know this?" demanded Vassalluzzo.

"Easy," said the broker. "I just called Larry Pacey." Pacey was a marketing executive who had left Office Depot to work at Office Warehouse. "I posed as a reporter from the *Philadelphia Business Journal* and said we wanted to do a story on his opening in Philadelphia and, particularly, on his new sites," continued the broker. Pacey told the broker that the information was highly confidential, but that he would check to see if he could release the information because the company might want the publicity. Permission granted. "We now knew where all sites were," says Stemberg, "so we checked them out. It turned out the sites were just God-awful. We said, 'Look, this will be great. Let 'em come.' "

Hot competition instantaneously transformed some friendships into enmity. Stemberg had formed a close relationship with Mark Begelman, CEO of Office Club in California, almost from the company's inception in 1987. Begelman hadn't conceived the idea for Office Club—he had been recruited from the furniture store industry to office supplies retailing by venture capitalists eager to get a

TODD KRASNOW

"Looking back, the market was so much bigger than anybody thought it was going to be that we probably invested way more energy than we should have in worrying about competitors. The industry has proven to be one of the best segments of retailing that there is, with loads of opportunity for everyone. To think that we were worrying about each other when we had three Staples stores and they had two Office Depot stores, with hindsight, was the wrong thing to pay attention to."

piece of this hot new concept. But he adapted beautifully. "He really understands the nuts and bolts of retailing, store presentation, visual merchandising, and advertising," says Steve Westerfield, who was running WORKplace at the time.

With Staples on the East Coast and Office Club on the West Coast, normal competitive instincts were muffled. Stemberg and Begelman attended each other's store openings, got to know each other's wives and traded ideas. "We were somewhat cautious. We didn't open the kimono all the way, but we would compare notes on how to compete with Office Depot—who was sort of the enemy," says Stemberg.

Then Staples received a flood of capital when it went public. After watching Office Depot operate so effortlessly in its low-cost markets, Stemberg and his team made a momentous decision: It would enter the Los Angeles market. "Office Depot was doing so well because they could afford to advertise heavily. They were in cheap markets. I couldn't buy the *New York Times* or *New York Newsday*. Those guys could go to Orlando and buy the paper dirt cheap in those days, and bang—open three stores," says

Stemberg. But costs on the West Coast were high, as they were on the East Coast. Staples hoped it could create another "fortress" there. "It entered L.A.," says Stemberg. And that was the end of his friendship with Begelman. "He hated me for it," says Stemberg.

Real-Life Lesson

The lines of battle change constantly. *Territory is everything in Staples' business. Even if the borders in your business aren't the kind that can be drawn on a map, they exist. Do not assume they won't be infringed upon by competitors—or that you can't cross them yourself. And don't assume your relationships will stay the same if the boundaries change.*

May 1, 1986—founders Tom Stemberg (left) and Leo Kahn at the grand opening of the first Staples store in Brighton, Massachusetts. Leo and Tom, who pioneered the $14-billion office superstore industry, were initially rivals in the supermarket industry before becoming cofounders of Staples.

April 1987—Tom and Leo celebrating the grand opening of the third Staples store in Providence, Rhode Island. Little did they know that Staples would grow to be the sixth company in U.S. history to achieve $3 billion in annual sales within 10 years of start-up.

Staples successful formula was simple: cut the cost of office supplies in half.

February 1988—Staples brings the savings to New York. Celebrating the grand opening of the first Staples Office Superstore in Manhattan are (left to right) Dinny Starr, Una Finn, Demos Parneros, Suzanne Gramaglia, Alan Berkowitz, and John Hughes.

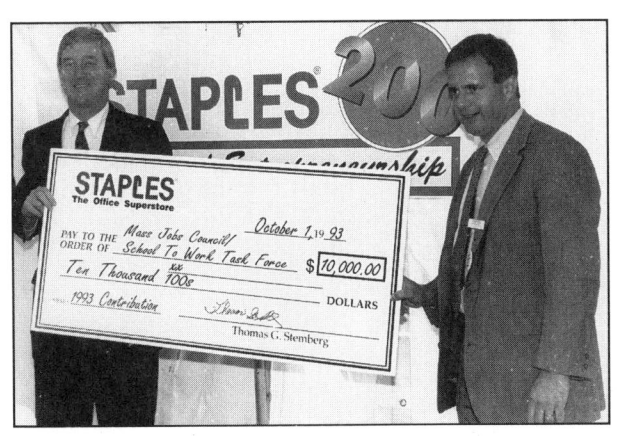

October 1993—Staples opens its 200th store in Newton, Massachusetts. Governor Bill Weld (left) congratulates Tom Stemberg. By Staples 10th anniversary date (May 1, 1996), Staples will have more than 500 superstores and 25,000 associates worldwide.

Staples' Board of Directors (1996)—(Back row, left to right) Jim Moody, Row Moriarty, Mitt Romney, and Larry Heisey. (Seated) Bob Nakasone, Leo Kahn, Tom Stemberg, Betsy Burton, and Marty Trust. (Not pictured) Paul Walsh and Dave Lubrano.

6 NEW YORK AND OTHER FOREIGN CITIES

Strictly speaking, Staples didn't become an international company until 1993. But it learned how to enter strange lands with foreign customs by opening stores in the daunting city of New York. "The retail real estate market in North America is in many ways a jungle—and in New York it's a heightened jungle," says Joe Vassalluzzo. All the rules that applied to real estate transactions in New England were suspended in The Big Apple.

Landlords run the gamut in race, religion, and disposition. "The Mob is our landlord in at least half a dozen sites. There's a lot of it in New York and you sort of get used to it," Stemberg says. Myra Hart, Staples' first head of real estate operations, remembers trying to negotiate for a derelict property owned by Iranians. Though they were all sitting at the same table, she could not get the Iranians to speak to her during the negotiations. "They would address everything to the men," she recalls. To reach an agreement, she had to periodically ask the landlords to leave the room, so that she could direct her colleagues about handling the discussions.

Staples' Manhattan leases taught the company the first dictum of going global: When in alien territory, adapt to local customs. Stemberg, Hart, and Leo Kahn were reviewing the terms of one of the Manhattan deals in the Sixth Avenue office of Al Goldberg, their prospective landlord.

Goldberg's assistant was Ralph Marx, a gruff, cigar-chomping New Yorker who did not speak without Goldberg's permission. Hart asked how long it would take to get a permit.

Marx looked at Goldberg. Goldberg nodded. Marx turned to the Staples trio. "Rocko and Joe can get it for us in two to three weeks," he said in a heavy New York accent.

Hart was puzzled. "Excuse me. Who's Rocko and who's Joe?" she asked.

Marx looked at Goldberg. Goldberg nodded. Rolling a cigar from side to side in his mouth, Marx answered, "They're architectural expediters."

Hart didn't think she liked the sound of that. "No, you don't understand," she protested. "We're going to be a public company. We can't do anything close to breaking the law."

After a few minutes of listening to her objections, Goldberg leaned over and said in a condescending tone, "Toots, you don't understand how things get done in New York."

Affronted, Hart was about to jump to her feet when Kahn and Stemberg grabbed her arms to restrain her. Kahn leaned over and asked, "Tell me this now. How long would it take us—or would we even get a permit—if we didn't use an architectural expediter?"

Marx looked expectantly at Goldberg. Goldberg nodded. "Oh, about three years," said Marx.

At that point Kahn decided to strike a compromise. "Hey listen, Ralph ... Al ... what say you hire Rocko, you pay Rocko, and we pay you?" he suggested.

Adjusting to foreign customs does not mean caving on key negotiating points, however. Stemberg recalls flying to New York to meet with a potential landlord. As he and his real estate broker walked into the landlord's office building, the broker turned and said, "You know, I think the Mob may be the landlord here." After Stemberg and the broker concluded the meeting, Jack, the landlord, handed Stemberg a business card with an unfamiliar business name on it.

"What's this?" asked Stemberg.

"The family," intoned Jack.

"Which family?" wondered Stemberg.

"No, you idiot," roared Jack. *"The family!"*

Negotiations for the space later bogged down over the actual square footage involved. Because he was familiar with the store from its incarnation as a Finast supermarket, Stemberg knew the space measured 14,300 square feet—but Jack's documents described it as 15,000 square feet. Finally, Stemberg called Jack to say that Staples would only pay rent on the actual space.

"Look, the family thinks it's fifteen thousand square feet. You know?" Jack answered. "I'll make it fifteen thousand square feet for the rent we agreed on, or we can raise the rent on a lower square footage. Take your pick."

"Jack, you know we just can't do that. We've got banks involved in this. It's a fair rent for your building," responded Stemberg.

"Okay. Can we split the difference and call it fourteen six?" Jack asked.

Stemberg stuck to his guns and at the end of the day got the store for the agreed-upon rent—on 14,300 square feet. "They are among our best landlords," he says.

New Yorkers' sense of priorities was often wonderfully bizarre. In 1992, two supermarket entrepreneurs joined forces to buy a property in the Bay Ridge area of Brooklyn that had previously housed a supermarket. Though they were fierce competitors, the two characters wanted to ensure that this property would never, ever again become a supermarket. So they began negotiating with Staples. Early one morning, Joe Vassalluzzo showed up at a spartan, musty

Manhattan office to negotiate with them. It was early, so he asked for some coffee. That triggered a major argument. The coffee pot was broken and if the sole receptionist/secretary left the office to buy coffee, there would be no one to answer the phone. To Vassalluzzo's amazement, the two self-made entrepreneurs began to argue vehemently about who would go and who would pay. "We had a thirty-minute debate about coffee," remembers Vassalluzzo.

At that meeting the supermarket entrepreneurs insisted that their attorney be the scrivener. Vassalluzzo agreed. But within a few weeks of his return to Framingham, negotiations began to bog down. Why? The attorney was sick, said the supermarket owners. Vassalluzzo was skeptical. "A lot of times during negotiations there are hidden agendas," he explains. "So whenever something doesn't make sense you have to question it." As the months wore on, and the attorney's illness continued to be the ostensible reason, Vassalluzzo and his team questioned the explanation so often that even the supermarket owners began to doubt whether their attorney was sick.

Finally, nine months after negotiations had started, the transaction was consummated. Normally, you do not hear from a landlord after the lease is signed. But one day Vassalluzzo received a call from one of the supermarket owners. Remember all the months that the attorney was sick? he asked Vassalluzzo. Well, the attorney had died. The New Yorker paused. Then he reflected soberly about how important it was for everyone to remember to stop and smell the roses in life. Joe had no sooner murmured his agreement than the landlord, without missing a beat, began to rake Vassalluzzo over the coals regarding a tax bill. "I said, 'Wait a minute. What about smelling the roses . . . ?'" says Vassalluzzo with a laugh.

The other supermarket owner was equally proficient at

ingratiating himself while serving his own interests. He called Vassalluzzo one day and asked if Staples had noticed that it was missing trolleys from its store. After finally realizing that the supermarket owner was talking about shopping carts, Vassalluzzo demurred, saying that he wasn't in a position to know. "Well," the supermarket owner informed him as though he were doing Vassalluzzo a huge favor, "one of our supermarket employees has been stealing trolleys from Staples. We are going to terminate the employee and return the carts to Staples," the supermarket owner continued.

"Gee," said Vassalluzzo. "That's very nice of you."

"I just want you to know I'm doing you a service," the entrepreneur replied. Then he added, almost as an afterthought, "Yeah, our meat manager was stealing meat from the supermarket and using your carts to carry it away." That, Vassalluzzo came to believe, was how New Yorkers defined selflessness.

On another occasion, Staples was pursuing a former disco on Queens Boulevard. Joe, the owner, was having difficulty relating to Katherine McGlade, a Staples real estate director. He wanted to make a special demand, man to man, so he invited Henry Flieck, head of real estate, to an evening of women's mud wrestling. Flieck declined, so Joe, a balding, well-dressed man in his forties, made his pitch to Flieck after dinner in a dark Queens restaurant instead. What he needed was money—$500,000. Normally, a tenant is not required to make a down payment on a lease. But Joe was tormented for reasons he did not explain and wanted cash from Staples.

"Look, we've got to sign today," Joe wheedled, leaning over the table. "I don't care if we sign—just give me even $100,000 today. Henry, we're friends. We ate together. We drank together. We have a relationship. I need the money today."

"It was like a scene out of a Scorsese movie. He literally wanted a huge cash payment with no security," recalls Vassalluzzo. Staples did not give him the money, and the former disco became a Korean food market.

Some of Staples' most memorable New York moments came out of a relationship with one of the country's largest and most successful real estate entrepreneurs. Vassalluzzo first met this powerful landlord regarding a lease Staples had purchased in northern New Jersey back when Staples was still a smallish company. The ostensible reason for the meeting was to discuss the possibility of Staples selling the lease back to the landlord and releasing it from them, an arrangement the landlord favored because it would give him more control.

The real reason was that Vassalluzzo, who had recently joined Staples, would try to get a major concession from the landlord: renewal options. Thus far the landlord's company had not granted Staples the standard option to renew the lease after ten years at its own discretion. "I was there to demonstrate that Staples had made a tremendous commitment to its growth program by recruiting high-level professionals and that Staples was a serious player," says Vassalluzzo. "All of which meant nothing to this guy."

The landlord did not listen to anything Vassalluzzo had to say. Instead he began to talk about the nice relationship building between Staples and his own organization. He mentioned the number of deals they had made together. Then, seemingly talking to his chief operating officer, who was also in the room, the landlord mentioned a property in another spot in New Jersey. "Oh, West Paterson," he exclaimed to his associate while keeping his eyes locked on Vassalluzzo. "That's the lease where we can throw them out any time we want!"

Being terminated at the landlord's will is the last thing

any tenant wants—and it would be a humiliation for Staples to have to accept such a condition. The landlord knew Vassalluzzo was new. "He wanted to see what kind of a reaction I would have. I was floored, but I said, 'I can't believe you have a right to do that. I haven't read the lease, but it would be startling to me if that were true,'" recalls Vassalluzzo. After holding his ground in the meeting, Vassalluzzo was surprised upon his return to Framingham to find that if he terminated all the tenants in the mall, the landlord did indeed have the right to terminate Staples, too.

Real-Life Lesson

Doing business in foreign cities is foreign. *It's obvious, but no one is really prepared for when it happens to them. To accomplish anything in an alien culture you'll have to bend at least a few rules. The trick is to know which principles you are willing to amend and which you aren't—and why.*

Going International: An Unnecessary Diversion?

While Staples coped with the mad rush of clones in the U.S., a Canadian businessman was beginning to picture a chain of office supply superstores in his country. As president of Beaver Lumber, which was owned by the Molsen brewing company, Jack Bingleman had in 1989 initiated a large research project that evaluated the prospects of starting a Home Depot–like chain in Canada. Molsen ultimately launched a home center chain, which was later sold to Home Depot. But from the beginning, Bingleman was more strongly attracted to the idea of super-large discount stores than to the home center business. "In the process of doing the research, I became extremely convinced that big-box category killers were going to play a big role in the future, and I became interested in the idea as both a retailer and an investor," recalls Bingleman. He did not have to look far to see what kind of product might work in the superstore setting. Molsen also owned one of Canada's two largest office supply chains. That business was a creature of the past, as Bingleman saw it: inefficient, with high-priced merchandise.

Bingleman was so excited about the opportunity that in 1990 he quit Beaver to research the new business. He also contacted Staples, Office Club, and Office Depot, hoping to plug into a proven formula that was up and running. After Mike Grossman, one of Staples' first directors, introduced him to Stemberg, Bingleman felt he'd found his corporate sponsor. "I liked Tom. I liked Staples, and in particular I liked it because they did business adjacent to Canada and had distribution facilities that were somewhat close to the Canadian border."

But did Staples like Bingleman and his idea? Stemberg

did. He had no ambivalence about the opportunity that Bingleman was presenting. Here was Bingleman, an experienced, successful retailer, who wanted to be the first office supplies superstore chain in Canada, just as Staples had been in the U.S. Bingleman wanted Staples to share its expertise, but he was willing to finance his start-up without Staples. What did Staples have to lose by supporting him?

The board, however, felt quite differently. Staples had established only thirty-five or so stores and the competition from clones was fierce. Staples had opportunities aplenty in its own country—the total market was beginning to look as if it could hit $100 billion. Canada's market was only about $10 billion. The last thing Staples needed was to divert capital and energy to a start-up in another country, argued Dave Lubrano and other board members. "It was very difficult for people born and raised in the U.S. to understand the poten-

JACK BINGLEMAN, PRESIDENT, NORTH AMERICAN SUPERSTORES

"It's very important that you run all these businesses with the same computer hardware and software and financial systems. Therefore you have to have things like system steering committees. Or you have to have merchandising forums in which you can have idea transfers. You can get involved in exchanging the best practices between countries. For example, not all great ideas came from the States. The team in Canada became quick believers in selling computer hardware, printers, software—that side of our business—and drove it very hard. Staples picked up on that. It's good for both businesses when you have these units that have some degree of freedom. They develop good ideas, good initiatives, that you can then take advantage of back here."

tial of globalization. Being a European and having traveled a lot, Tom had a different perspective," says Steve Westerfield. Stemberg refused to give up and, finally, in late 1990 the board agreed to a tentative first step: Staples would split the research costs with Bingleman while he developed a business plan that could be used to raise capital and recruit talent. After the business plan was written, Staples would decide whether or not it would become an investor.

By the time Bingleman was finished with his plan, the board agreed to invest $2 million for 16 percent ownership of the Canadian's business. During the first half of 1991, Goldman Sachs lined up twenty-five individual and institutional investors willing to put up $10 million. By fall, the company, named Business Depot, was ready to open its first store.

Staples' first baby step into globalization was tremendously useful in laying the groundwork for future cross-border expansion. Though the Canadian market was very similar to its U.S. counterpart, it was different enough that Staples had to learn how to amend its U.S. blueprint for success. "Ninety-five percent of what you do and the way customers respond in Canada is the same as the U.S.," says Bingleman. "But you can get into a lot of trouble with the other five percent."

Take the simple logistics of getting the product into the stores. Canada is a country in which everybody lives a hundred miles from the U.S. border and that stretches thirty-five hundred miles from coast to coast. Everything moves east and west. In the U.S., by contrast, things move north, south, east, west, and in circles. That single difference dictated an array of differences in how Business Depot would operate. It meant Bingleman's operation required a completely different distribution system than Staples. It was a key factor in electing whether to use local, regional, or national advertising.

There were myriad other differences, too. Two languages are spoken in Canada. Electrical equipment requires a different approval process in Canada. According to Bingleman, "Canadian managers are more intuitive than Americans. Americans are far more analytical. The reason for that is that if you want to be a national chain in Canada, you have to operate in a market like Toronto, where there are four million people and you have to operate in little communities in Saskatchewan, where there are two thousand people. You can't put the Coke machine in the same place in every store, because they're so different."

But perhaps the most important element of Staples' Canadian experiment is that it learned how crucial a strong relationship is to international operations. Staples' success in the U.S., and the proliferation of competitors, had fostered a cookie-cutter approach to fast growth. For the first time, its executives had to live with a partner, Bingleman, who had a strong point of view, too. Though Staples was very much in the driver's seat because it had the expertise and clout in banking, leasing, and legal matters, it was forced to develop methods to share—and receive—the information. "You learn how to manage these relationships because you probably need the relationship to understand what the country is all about, what the culture is all about, and how to do business," explains Bingleman.

Stemberg's foresight in sponsoring Business Depot was richly rewarded. Business Depot stores usually began turning a profit within ten months of opening. Within two and a half years, the company had nearly thirty stores and began to produce earnings. By 1994, its market share of the Canadian office products industry surpassed Grand and Toy, the previous industry leader. Staples, which had been boosting its ownership in the intervening years, decided to buy the rest of Business Depot. "The Canadian operation was more successful than Office Depot or OfficeMax in its formative years because of the advice Staples gave it," says Westerfield. "Jack worked unrelentingly and the company has gained such strong control of the Canadian market that if anybody wants to be a meaningful competitor up there, it will be costly for them."

Real-Life Lesson

Think three steps ahead. *With perspective, particularly twenty-twenty hindsight, everything seems clear. But sometimes being swamped by the particulars of a current business can give you extraordinary foresight. Being in the midst of a battle for dominance of the U.S. market allowed Stemberg to see how to wage that war even more successfully in another country. There he could execute the concept even better—raising more money sooner, blanketing the country faster, and forestalling competitors more effectively. In pondering the shape of the battle* **outside** *of the U.S., somewhere in the distant future, he was thinking three steps ahead. If he had limited his thinking to the all-consuming present, Staples would have never become Canada's industry leader.*

Speed Bumps on the Transatlantic Highway

Staples' forays into Canada brought a dazzlingly seductive issue before the board: foreign expansion. None of the company's rivals had stepped foot in other countries yet. If Staples charged ahead, it could potentially "own" the industry in other countries. The board was also concerned about sales growth. After presenting shareholders with 50 percent annual sales growth, what would Staples do for an encore once the U.S. market was saturated with office supplies superstores?

The answer seemed to point to Europe. The U.K., for example, seemed ripe for the Staples concept. Individual and business customers were being served by small, high-priced mom-and-pop shops offering little service. But there was no Jack Bingleman setting up a chain in Britain. What Staples needed, concluded Stemberg and his directors, was a corporate partner in the U.K. According to Joe Vassalluzzo, "You absolutely cannot do it yourself. There are too many cultural impediments for you to know where the booby traps lie. In a retail start-up the most important task is to generate locations. There's no way a U.S. national can go into any country and generate the real estate it needs. That person will be chasing his tail for a long time." After months of research and networking, Staples in 1992 joined forces with Kingfisher, plc., a large retailer that operates home improvement, consumer electronics, and Woolworth chains in Britain.

Because both countries are English-speaking, the temptation is to believe that there will be few impediments to transferring a U.S. business to the U.K. But, in Vassalluzzo's estimation, George Bernard Shaw was right: The U.S. and Britain are two great countries separated by a common language. He remembers the day that he overheard a U.K. associate talking to a Staples associate about turnover. The Staples associate grew more and more perplexed until Vassalluzzo interrupted to clarify matters. In the U.S. "turnover" refers to "employee churn." In Britain, it means "sales." Says Vassalluzzo, "Multiply that misunderstanding a hundred times and you have some idea of what it's like—and that's in a country with the same language."

TODD KRASNOW

"I went to a closing in Germany that shows you how big the cultural differences are. I took the red-eye, flew all night, didn't sleep particularly much and then went to their offices. For some reason the office buildings in Hamburg don't have particularly good ventilation and everybody smokes in Germany. We went into this room. Under German law the documents have to be read out loud before you can sign them. So, we had to stay for six hours in a smoke-filled room, with only little biscuits to eat and wine to drink. I'm into my twenty-eighth hour of being awake.

Then came the closing dinner. We went to a restaurant in a nice section of Hamburg and the first course that came around was a soup. It was just a broth, and the first thing the waiter did was crack an egg into each one. The soup was not warm enough for the egg to cook—it was just sitting there. Then they came around and scraped these little red things into the soup, which were bone marrow. This is like nine o'clock at night and the only thing I've had to eat all day is beer and schnapps, so I'm famished. Then the main course came, which our host ordered for us. It was a house specialty: pig knuckle. I am so tired because I have not had a chance to take out my contact lenses and my eyes feel like they're going to fall out of my head. This is my recollection of doing business in Germany. It is a wholly different culture and you don't think of it as being that different."

Nevertheless, results from Staples U.K.'s four pilot stores have justified the expansion. While they're still not profitable, revenues are stronger than the company expected. So in 1996 Staples will bring its total to thirty-five stores, hoping to snare a significant portion of the country's $10 billion market before Globus, its only rival, expands its presence.

Staples' decision to enter Germany in 1992 was guided by what seemed like a custom-made opportunity: a chance to buy into MAXI-Papier, a clone company that was copying what Staples had done in the U.S. The German company's first store was doing well. "We said, 'Look, let's just buy into their business with the rights to step up our ownership over time,'" recalls Stemberg.

No sooner were the papers signed than the problems began to mount. Subsequent stores were located in poor spots and did not perform as well. The stores themselves were, on average, fifteen thousand square feet and carried four thousand items. The smaller size and smaller selection robbed MAXI-Papier stores of some of the key features offered by their U.S. cousins. But even more important, business conditions in Germany are positively daunting for a retailer touting low prices and convenience. The country prohibits companies from offering a coupon worth more than about twenty-five cents. It is illegal to say that you have guaranteed low prices because German law is very paternalistic. Retailers are not allowed to be open after 6:00 P.M. except on Thursdays. "We can't do many of the things that have worked for us in the U.S. So how do you build your business?" asks Todd Krasnow.

Staples' natural response to MAXI-Papier's troubles was to try something gutsy, and if that didn't work, try something else. But here is where cultural differences began to seem like impenetrable walls. "From their perspective,

Americans change their mind all the time about everything. They think we should just slow down and in five years we'll have a very nice business," explains Krasnow. Each partner also believes their own expertise should dictate the course of the business. "They think we don't understand their market," says Stemberg. "We'd send guys over on joint venture teams to accomplish X,Y and Z and the German guys would say, 'Oh, yeah, we'll do that, sure.' Then after the team went home they'd say, 'Should we do it? Nah . . . They won't be back for awhile.'"

The copy center debate was a key example. None of the stores that Staples inherited when it bought a 48 percent interest in MAXI-Papier had copy machines available to customers. They had always been a successful component of Staples' U.S. stores, so the company naturally suggested that copy centers be introduced in Germany. "The managing director said there is no way the German customer is interested in using copy centers," remembers Vassalluzzo. But after months and months of negotiations,

Tom Stemberg

"When things don't work out, a leader should be willing to take the blame. Most people running companies could do it. It's a wonderful leadership technique. So many companies are absorbed with covering up their mistakes and rationalizing their bad decisions. It's just much better to say, 'Hey we screwed that one up. Next . . .' When Germany was going badly, I made a big point of making Germany my project. It would have been very easy to slough it off and blame everybody else. By saying, 'Hey, we tried Germany. Right now it's not working. Let's own up to it. Let's deal with it,' we made it pretty clear that it's not the end of the world to try something and have it fail."

Staples prevailed. MAXI-Papier would test a center. The result? It was an immediate success.

Such victories were too few, though. By mid-1994, the board was considering writing off its investment in MAXI-Papier. In the end, however, Stemberg and Vassalluzzo decided to extend the experiment with new management. They brought in Peter von le Fort as managing director. He was one of the original investors in MAXI-Papier and former chief operating officer of Max Bahr, one of Germany's leading home improvement chains. They also promoted Michael Bauer, a German national trained by both IKEA and Staples in the U.S., to operations controller of the German operation. While the moves have improved Staples' ability to implement new ideas, the company does not expect Germany to generate significant earnings until the end of the decade.

Real-Life Lesson

A solid working relationship is more important than any other factor to being successful in international markets. *An overseas business must pass other criteria, of course. But an international venture won't fly just because the market for low-priced office supplies is big and untapped, for example. You need a partner with whom you can truly work well. Sometimes the only way to be sure of that is to insist that one partner be in the driver's seat. "I don't know if a fifty-fifty joint venture is the way to go. There has to be one decisive party at the end of the day," says Joe Vassalluzzo.*

7 RACE OF THE RETAILERS

Though it had been invaded by an army of clones early in life, Staples did not feel the heat of burning competition until it broke into the southern California market with four stores in 1990. With eight stores already established, Office Club, the leading competitor, was hardly likely to ignore this incursion into its territory. Moreover, Mark Begelman, Office Club's CEO and a onetime ally of Stemberg's, felt betrayed by Staples' entry into his territory. A conflagration was inevitable.

But at first Staples ignored Office Club. Instead, it was scrutinizing Price Club. Though it was a warehouse store selling food and general merchandise, not a Staples-style store, Price Club had the largest share of the office supplies market in California. So Staples' marketing campaign focused tightly on the advantages of shopping at Staples over Price Club: It had the same low prices but more merchandise and no membership fee. "What we failed to realize was that Price Club was very worried about Office Club—and was pricing against Office Club," says Krasnow. "So when we went and matched Price Club, we were matching Office Club. And Office Club was saying, 'We're not going to let anybody have the same price as us.'"

The war began. Office Club lowered their prices, causing Price Club to drop prices. Staples, in turn, followed Price Club down. Begelman could tolerate Price Club having the same prices as his company, but not Staples. So

Todd Krasnow

"The notion of fighting with each other over price is actually kind of ludicrous. But at the time you're so intent on establishing yourself and not letting anybody, any competitor get any headway. There was no particular reason to lower prices, from a competitive point of view, but it was a very difficult process to break. That price-cutting cycle repeated itself several times early on as competitors converged in different parts of the country. Every time it happened there would be this drop, drop, drop, drop and then it would start to go back up, leveling out at prices slightly below where they started. We in the industry didn't get more rational until 1992. We finally realized that it's not in any company's self-interest to have a price war because you can get lots of market share without having a price war. And having a price war among low-priced competitors doesn't get you more market share. It didn't serve any purpose."

he knocked prices down again. And on and on it went. "It was one of those terrifying plunges, where prices just kept going down and down and down and, in reality, there was no particular reason for it," remembers Krasnow. The price war drove margins down by a steep 7 or 8 percent.

The grand irony: the pain was entirely self-inflicted by all three stores. Price Club had ten area locations, but only around two hundred office supply items. Between them, Staples and Office Club had just twelve stores in all of southern California. They were so new to the market that there was plenty of business for everyone. They were just beginning to take market share away from stationery stores and dealers. Retail customers were just beginning to discover them. There was very little chance that customers would drive away from their store to a competitor's because of a small price difference. No matter where the retailers stood in relation to each other, all of the prices looked good to customers who had been paying 100 percent more!

After three or four months, Staples finally came to its senses. "We realized by engaging in this price war we were focusing on our competitors, not our customers. Our customers weren't paying attention to this spat," says Krasnow. So, with great trepidation, Staples raised its prices a little. "You feel like you're just doing the absolute wrong thing, because your whole position is: We have the lowest price," says Krasnow. But Office Club and Price Club followed, and the cycle reversed itself. Eventually the three companies carved out different price niches, each unwilling to be beat on twenty or so top-selling items.

Real-Life Lesson

There can be more than one winner. *The heat of competition can cause you to concentrate on your enemies instead of your customers. Staples and Office Club were tearing the profits out of their businesses when they did not need to. Today there are 130 office supply superstores prospering in southern California. Some belong to Staples. Some to others. If the market is big enough, there is room enough for more than one winner.*

Guerrilla Warfare

Plentiful as business was for the newly hatched office supplies chains, some battles with competitors had to be fought. In an incident well-known in the industry, Steve Westerfield, the former CEO of WORKplace who eventually sold his company to Staples, was forced into waging one with Office Depot. WORKplace was a clone that had built up a strong presence in California and Florida not long after Staples began operating. But it was so undercapitalized that by 1989 it was forced into selling assets. "Already Staples and Office Depot had huge critical mass. If you don't ramp up a start-up as fast as competitors do, then it loses much of its value," says Westerfield. So WORKplace sold its California stores—Staples turned down the chance to buy them—and used the assets to expand its inventory and to add six stores to the four it already had established in the Tampa Bay region.

Though WORKplace was still a speck compared with Office Depot, it began to develop a terrific business in Florida. It was the first clone to expand heavily into consumer electronics. As WORKplace sales began to grow impressively, Office Depot took notice. It had no stores in the Tampa area and decided to make an offer to buy the upstart company. Westerfield and the board were insulted by the low buyout price that Office Depot proposed, according to industry sources. But Westerfield asked to meet David Fuente, Office Depot's CEO, to talk over the offer.

They met at the National Office Products Association show at McCormick Place, in Chicago. After finding a private booth, Westerfield sat down with Fuente and Steve Dougherty, Office Depot's president. Westerfield's point to the two executives was simple: WORKplace's investors would consider selling the company, but it was worth much more. As he explained how the WORKplace stores were progressing, Fuente listened closely and Dougherty tensely chain-smoked cigarettes. Then, say sources familiar with the incident, Dougherty jumped to his feet. "If you think we're going to allow you to make profits in these Florida stores, you've got another thing coming!" A few minutes later, he left the room. Fuente looked embarrassed. Conversation became strained. Though they had decided on nothing, Westerfield reminded Fuente before they parted that WORKplace still had an interest in further discussions.

Two weeks later, Office Depot rolled out the cannons. It opened its first store in Tampa and unleashed an aggressive advertising campaign. Full-page newspaper ads screamed the news: Everything in Office Depot cost 15 percent less than in WORKplace. Westerfield called Fuente and pointed out that the campaign's claims weren't true. Fuente seemed willing to look into the matter. But the ads continued. Office Depot next published its store catalog. Pictured on its cover were two hands ripping apart a WORKplace catalog. Office Depot's prices, the ad copy said, were 15 percent lower. Soon the picture became part of Office Depot's newspaper ads.

Westerfield protested to Fuente twice more. But the ads continued. Finally, he decided to take action. A small team of WORKplace managers bought fifty or sixty items from Office Depot's store. None of them sported prices below WORKplace's; in fact, they were more expensive. Westerfield took his beef to court, suing Office Depot for false advertising. Within ten days of the complaint being filed, Office Depot pulled its ads. Approximately six months later, a federal magistrate ruled in favor of WORKplace. The suit was finally settled out of court and a significant award was made to WORKplace, according to industry sources.

But Office Depot wasn't the least bit cowed by WORKplace. While still in litigation over advertising claims, Office

TODD KRASNOW

"Jack [Bingleman] grew up in Canadian business, was in real estate, and ended up being the CEO of the biggest home improvement chain in Canada. I can remember the early days of his starting Business Depot and Tom saying, 'You can't let Office Depot do X, Y, and Z.'" And Jack would say, 'Nobody would do that.' And time after time, Jack, who is very savvy and had been around the block a number of times, was amazed. He was used to a very gentlemanly game of how things work.

I remember there was one site where we had a deal with Beaver Lumber, his old company, to take on the lease. Everything was set. He had had lots of dealings with his old company, and the landlord, Conrad Black's Dominion stores. He had a letter of intent. Leases were being processed. And the next thing you know Office Depot had found a clause in the contract that said the owner could reclaim the site if the tenant found somebody to assign the lease to. So Office Depot went to the landlord and said, 'Hey, here's a half a million bucks. We want the site.' And they got it. The fact that somebody like Jack, who had a very big position in a big company, was taken aback by their aggressiveness says just how aggressive the industry is."

In the end, Bingleman did get $50,000 from Dominion stores for the trouble.

Depot rented a billboard in front of WORKplace's store on U.S. 19 North. Having just moved the company's offices into that store, Westerfield saw the billboard being prepped for painting. A call to the billboard company clued him in on Office Depot's move, and he quickly devised a counteroffensive play. The billboard was finally finished at 7:00 P.M. one night. "Office Depot," the billboard announced in ten-foot-tall letters, "Biggest selection, Better service, Low

Prices Guaranteed." But by 5:00 A.M. the next morning, Westerfield could look at the billboard with satisfaction. At his direction, a local landscaper had overnight planted five mature Florida palm trees directly in front of the billboard. Office Depot's message was unreadable. Tampa's newspapers, radio, and television stations loved the story—and invented their own jokes to go with it. Maybe Office Depot should "leaf" town, one reporter concluded.

The stakes in Jack Bingleman's battle against Office Depot in Canada were even higher: his company's identity in the minds of customers. When Bingleman launched his company, Staples' board was confident enough of his prospects to become investors, but it did not want to put Staples name on a business that it did not control. So Bingleman came up with a list of possible names and settled on Business Depot. Immediately, Bingleman began the tedious process of having the name registered, in order for it to gain trademark status. The protocol, which can take years to finish, involved having the Canadian government publish the name, which it did, and waiting for a period of time during which objections to the name can be filed by anyone who chooses to do so.

Not long after Business Depot began opening stores in 1991, Office Depot acquired the Great Canadian Office Supply Warehouse, a retail chain. For a few months, the Florida company operated the chain under its original name. Then it began to change the store names to Office Depot. It was an extraordinarily threatening strategy. Office Depot sounded confusingly similar to Business Depot. "By the time they entered our territory, we had brought a lot of equity into the business. And we had to some degree become famous by having great selection and bringing prices down. So we didn't want someone else to come in and take advantage with look-alike merchandise and look-alike stores," explains Bingleman. But the real menace did not appear until early 1992 when Office Depot challenged Bingleman's right to use the Business Depot name. Losing its name would mean losing its relationships with customers—in short, everything that matters in a retail business.

There were two pieces to the name issue. The first was Office Depot's challenge to the trademark. The only way to fight that was through the courts, which Bingleman began to do immediately. The second part involved common-law usage of names. When Office Depot began to enter the province of Ontario, where many of Business Depot's stores were located, Bingleman asked a judge to rule on whether or not the company could use the Depot name.

He had ample evidence supporting his case. The judge granted Business Depot an injunction against Office Depot. The Florida company could not use its name in eastern Canada. Because it had already begun to erect Office Depot signs over some stores, the company hurriedly covered the word *Depot* with tarps. "We started calling them 'Office Tarp,'" remembers advertising vice president Phyllis Wasserman. The trademark legal battle was still continuing in 1995, but the injunction was a critical victory for Staples.

Real-Life Lessons

Pick your battles. *Aggressiveness for its own sake is wasted energy. But fighting a threat that truly matters is paramount. Don't let a competitor's size prevent you from responding. Tiny WORKplace prevailed by pursuing legal redress. But a lawsuit isn't your only option. Westerfield's landscape caper not only turned the tables on Office Depot, it won WORKplace invaluable publicity.*

8 THE PRICE OF SUCCESS: GLORY AND INFAMY

For most entrepreneurs, taking their company public is the Holy Grail. An initial public offering, or IPO, betokens acceptance by the financial community and credibility among its corporate peers. It turns company founders into multimillionaires. But for Tom Stemberg, the main reason to go public in the spring of 1989 was to maximize shareholders' value. He also understood the great trick to raising capital: It's better to get funding when your company is hot than to wait until you need it.

There were lots of other options. Stemberg had regularly fielded offers from would-be financiers and buyers, almost from the company's inception. But the office supplies industry was heating up on Wall Street. A robust stock market was warmly embracing one new public company after another. Investment bankers had been making regular pilgrimages to Staples' headquarters, clamoring to be allowed to underwrite the company's going-public deal. Both Office Depot and Office Club now traded on the stock exchanges. Investors were so excited about the sector that one company, HQ Office Supplies Warehouse, successfully sold its shares to the public without having generated a drop of revenue. And Staples, the company that had invented the industry, had just logged its first quarter of profits. It was time.

Stemberg was as rigorously analytical in choosing his

investment bankers as he had been in picking venture capital partners. He was determined to use Staples' IPO as a springboard for further increasing the company's value and growth prospects. And he refused to take chances with a firm that could not deliver multiple benefits to Staples. "You can get screwed really badly when you go public," says Staples director Dave Lubrano. "The tendency is to go talk to one or two investment bankers and then be at their mercy."

Stemberg began his research by grilling investment banks' customers. Who better to assess how investment banks executed initial public offerings than the folks who bought the stock of these just-public companies? Stemberg asked money management firms such as State Street Research, Fidelity, and Kemper to rate the investment banks' credibility and research analysts.

The quality of a firm's research analysts was paramount. Wall Street analysts, who recommend stocks to large institutional investors, could have a huge impact on how well the stock performed after it went public. The best analysts' confidence in a company could keep its stock trading at high levels for years. Moreover, Stemberg knew that if an analyst's firm underwrote Staples' IPO, the analyst was then obliged to cover and report on the company. "Ultimately I wanted the bank to tell the Staples story to investors and that's mainly a function of the analysts they have," explains Stemberg.

After polling investment banks' customers, he turned to the firms themselves. "Most companies (about to go public) don't do their homework when it comes to investment bankers," says Bo Cheadle, the Montgomery Securities analyst who began visiting Staples in 1988. "Tom interviewed virtually every investment banker in the U.S." John Berg, a managing director at Montgomery, remembers receiving four pages of questions about Montgomery's initial public offerings experience. Among the questions: How would the firm value Staples? How have the firm's IPOs performed? What are the firm's biggest accounts? Which of the firm's research analysts cover retailing? What are their records? And on and on they went. It took Montgomery six days to collect the answers. But that was only the beginning of what Stemberg wanted to know. "There were two or three requests for additional information, culminating in a formal presentation to Staples," says Berg. "This was hands down the most intensive selection process of investment bankers known to mankind."

By late 1988, Stemberg had anointed his team of bankers. William Blair, a Chicago firm that scored extremely well in Stemberg's rating system, would comanage the deal with Montgomery. While the San Francisco firm hadn't ranked quite as high as Blair, Montgomery held a small company conference every year that was one of the two best in the country. Staples would be well-served by becoming a showpiece on that stage, Stemberg believed. Staples awarded the lead management position to Goldman Sachs, the Tiffany's of investment banking.

Then the fun began. Going public is the financial and legal equivalent of stringing up your underwear for everyone to examine. And the examination is endless. "It's an immense amount of work. I can never describe how difficult it was while also trying to run and nurture the business," says Bob Leombruno. To negotiate the terms of the deal, Stemberg and his top executives huddled with the bankers and lawyers in Staples' run-down 150 California Street headquarters. "This building was decrepit, with little heat. We used to joke about the rats joining us at our meetings. We couldn't complain though, because Staples needed to have the lowest cost structure in the industry," says Berg.

The jokes dried up during the next step: preparing the offering prospectus, a document describing the company, which is filed with the Securities and Exchange Commission and given to potential investors. Drafting sessions, as they are called, are among the most tedious time-wasters an executive ever encounters. In addition to Stemberg and his executives, accountants, investment bankers, and lawyers from the two firms crowded into the conference room of Staples' law firm for twelve- to fourteen-hour meetings. The sessions entailed hours of endless questioning by the lawyers and bankers who wanted reassurance that they were not misrepresenting the tiniest detail to investors. "How can we be sure that there won't be an eminent domain event on this site?" "Can you give me comfort that there's no risk of obsolescent inventory?" Says Stemberg, "They just waste hours of time, and management gets sucked into it." At ten o'clock one evening, the exhausted group sat around a littered conference table. Gary Balter, an investment banker from Goldman Sachs who was such an avid hockey fan that he scheduled drafting sessions around Boston Bruins hockey games, portentously asked to be left alone in the room with the Staples managers. His question concerned Staples' landlords. "He said, 'Let me ask you a very difficult question. Our investigations show that one of your landlords is a convicted felon. Does that surprise you?'" says Stemberg. "I said, 'Not whatsoever. What surprises me is that there's only one.'"

Once the offering documents were filed with the Securities and Exchange Commission, Stemberg and his bankers embarked upon the most critical piece of going public: whetting investors' appetites for Staples stock. They left on a seventeen-day "road show," traveling around the world to present the company to potential investors. A normal road show has a hellish schedule, as bankers try to

Tom Stemberg

"My mother-in-law had an M.B.A. from Wharton and was a very savvy investor. Now her son-in-law was taking his company public and she planned to buy a thousand shares in it—a big investment. So she tells me she wants to attend one of the road show meetings. I'm worried that she might want to attend the really big one that everyone attends in New York at the Waldorf Astoria. I asked Goldman Sachs, 'Are we going to make a stop in Philadelphia?' The bankers said no. I said that we should go. So after meeting T. Rowe Price in Baltimore we get on a Metroliner to go to Philadelphia and have lunch at the Four Seasons Hotel. There were about twenty potential investors, venture capitalists, and investment bankers there—plus my mother-in-law.

All of the Staples executives had been thoroughly grilled in how to respond to questions. If somebody asks you about a competitor, you say nice things, no matter how much you hate them. So one of the analysts from Delaware Management asks me how we compare ourselves with Office Depot. My answer was, 'They're a great company. Their approach is a little different from ours. They come from the lumber industry. We're supermarket guys. We believe in something else.' Toward the end of my answer I hear my mother-in-law's cane thumping on the floor. 'He's LYING,' she screamed out. 'I've been to the stores with him. That store is a dump. D-U-M-P!' It was one of those incredible moments. I put my arm around the Goldman Sachs banker and said, 'Aren't you glad we came to Philadelphia instead of New York?'"

squeeze in as much exposure to as many investors as possible into each twenty-four-hour period. Staples' road show was more brutal than most. "Tom is the Energizer

Bunny of finance—a road show warrior. He's willing to set as ambitious a schedule as possible," says John Wilson, Staples' chief financial officer. Investors had already heard that this was one IPO that should not be missed. "The presentations were absolutely packed," remembers Berg. "It was clearly what we all call a hot IPO."

The emotional pitch of these jam-packed days ranged from euphoric highs to oppressive lows. New York's classy Plaza Hotel was one of the last stops. Stemberg took the opportunity to make peace with Fred Adler, the venture capitalist who helped launch both Staples and its archrival, Office Depot. He invited Adler to sit up at the presenting table with the Staples executives and, in his speech, paid homage to Adler's sponsorship. Adler glowed. "I always try to kiss and make up with people," says Stemberg.

During one leg of the U.S. journey, Stemberg and Bob Spellman, Staples' senior vice president of finance at the time, missed their connection from Atlanta to Boston. Opting to get as close to home as possible, they caught a flight to Philadelphia instead, landing at the airport at one o'clock in the morning. There were no more flights to Boston and they were exhausted. But getting a hotel room for less than half a night's sleep would be frivolous. Stemberg curled up with his suitcase on a vinyl waiting room couch and conked out.

Selling the Staples story abroad brought Stemberg some of his best—and worst—moments. Starting in London, Michael Cohrs, a Goldman banker whom Stemberg had known at Harvard, put together a perfect day. Stemberg and his team stayed at the elegant Savoy Hotel and they met individually with investment giants, such as Mercury Warburg, throughout the morning and afternoon. The lunch presentation, to which the rest of the financial community was invited, was jammed. "Demand for the stock in London was wonderful," says Stemberg.

Full of excitement and high hopes, the Staples executives left for Switzerland at six o'clock the next morning. They met with a small group of potential investors at Goldman's Zurich office. Within minutes of the introductions, the Goldman banker in charge of selling Staples' stock asked a question that shocked Stemberg. How, he wondered, was Staples different from Price Club? And didn't it have the same business issues to wrestle with? Price Club, of course, was a grocery and general merchandise chain—a completely different animal, in other words. The question might have been acceptable if it had come from an investor. But here it was, coming from the mouth of a professional who was supposed to know Staples inside and out in order to sell the stock. Stemberg went ballistic. He started yelling and screaming at the Goldman banker. "Tom was ready to kill him and give Goldman the boot," according to John Berg.

Zurich had been a totally useless stop, but Stemberg and his crew were heartened when they returned to London, where orders for Staples stock continued to stream in, and boarded the Concorde. Arriving at JFK International Airport at 5:00 P.M., the executives lobbied USAir to board its 5:30 flight to Baltimore, instead of the 8:00 P.M. flight they had booked. While waiting, Stemberg returned a call from Bobby Haft, whose family owned and controlled Dart Drug. Haft told Stemberg he wanted to buy Staples. Stemberg wasn't interested in selling. As he hung up, he fretfully calculated whether or not Haft could mount a takeover attempt. No, he decided. Back at the gate, the Staples crew were given seats on the 5:30 flight.

A few hours earlier they had been jetting back from Europe on the Concorde. Now Stemberg found himself in the last row of a little turboprop with his knees jammed into the reclined seat in front of him. He thought his legs were going to fall off. Finally the plane landed. The fatigued Staples managers searched for the limousine that was supposed to ferry them to their hotel. It wasn't there. It turned out that one of their own investment bankers had snatched it. A taxi then, they thought. But it was Passover—most of the cabbies were on holiday. At last, after waking in London nearly twenty-four hours earlier, they found someone to take them to their hotel, where they collapsed from exhaustion.

The grueling work paid off. In late April, the road show was successfully completed and market conditions were perfect. In an ideal IPO, demand for the new stock far outstrips the supply. "You want it to be four to ten times the actual number of shares available," says Wilson. The price of a share of stock should be set high, so that as much money as possible is raised. But it can't be so high that the share price falls after the first day of trading.

JOHN WILSON

"You want the stock price to be high in an IPO because you want to maximize the proceeds to the company. But there are all kinds of other pricing pressures, too. Look at the 'spread' you pay the investment banks, which comes out of the proceeds from the IPO. We gave the bankers a high 'spread' of 7 percent because we wanted the bankers to feel good and have an incentive to make sure the deal is successful. This is particularly important over the long run because you want to come back to the market in the future. It's a fine balance that a CEO must strike. If you leave investors feeling happy, because the shares they bought at 19 are now trading at 25, they say, 'Yeah. I'll buy some more in the next round.'"

Investors' appetites for Staples' shares were so keen that the investment bankers had already reset the price range once. Initially set to come at $13 to $15 per share, the share price was revised to $15 to $18 per share before the final documents were filed with the SEC. Now demand from institutional investors was eight to ten times the supply of stock. The bankers decided to nudge the price up once more, to $19 per share. When the first Staples shares began trading, Stemberg was in his office trying to get back to work. It was tough to do. As the stock began floating up, Staples executives, whose shares in Staples were enriching them by the minute, kept popping into his office to report on the stock as it was bid up by enthusiastic investors. The stock surpassed $23 and closed at $22½, 18 percent above the offering price. Staples raised $61.7 million. "It was one of the fastest, most successful IPOs since the crash in 1987," says Wilson.

Real-Life Lesson

Don't stint on promotion for your IPO. *Stemberg and his team had a terrific story to tell, of course. But they also recognized that the stock price would benefit most by getting out there and telling the story rather than stinting on investment banker fees. "You're far better off paying the investment bankers a decent fee and feeding their enthusiasm for the deal than trying to nickel and dime them," says Stemberg. Justly or unjustly, an IPO's success has as much to do with showmanship and market buoyancy as with your company's true worth.*

Professional Naysayers Have Their Say

Though going public can make you rich, it can also subject you to slings and arrows whose sting is all the more painful because they are unwarranted. As a fast-growing company, Staples' stock was quickly awarded a high price-to-earnings multiple, meaning it usually traded at forty to fifty times its annual earnings per share. Though a high P/E is a positive sign of investors' happy expectations, it also makes a stock especially sensitive to even the slightest whisper of bad news. Why? Its high growth characteristics attract a breed of investors known as "momentum investors," who buy stocks with rapidly accelerating earnings and sell them on the tiniest of disappointments over a company's prospects. "Our stock is one of the most volatile in the market. Any slight concerns are multiplied and magnified," says John Wilson.

Staples learned how dramatically such concerns could hurt its standing in the financial community beginning in the fall of 1990. In late September, David Childe, an analyst with San Francisco–based Robertson Stephens & Co. who had been covering the office superstore industry for just over a year, issued a three-page report cutting his earnings estimates for companies in the industry. Such revisions can trigger a sharp sell-off as investors rush to bail out of a stock. This one felt particularly damaging. First it came as a complete surprise. Instead of alerting Staples of his change, as was customary, Childe simply faxed the report out to institutional investors. Second, the analyst recommended that investors not only sell the stock, but sell short—in other words, bet on the stock falling. Staples' stock had already been under pressure, falling from $25.50 in July to $16.00 just before Childe's report. It fell another 15 percent in the days following Childe's assessment that

Staples would be unable to crack the California market with profitable stores. All of this occurred while Childe was still publicly maintaining a "hold" rating on Staples' stock.

Surprised and angry, Stemberg and Spellman called Childe. If Childe didn't have the courtesy to alert Staples to his change of opinion, they told him, Staples would not have much interest in keeping him abreast of company developments.

A chagrined Childe quickly followed up the tense phone conversation with an apologetic letter. He agreed to notify Staples of any pending estimate changes and promised to supply the company with drafts of his research reports prior to publication. "Though we may differ at times, in no way would I ever intentionally undermine Staples' considerable achievements in the industry that you pioneered," he asserted in the letter.

The pattern of negative reports containing often-faulty reasoning continued for a month or two. Then Childe began faxing his early drafts, which Spellman or Stemberg corrected by faxed letter. A meeting with Childe and his boss, Michael Stark, in January had begun to ease the strain. But on February 19, 1991, Childe faxed a draft of a report in which he cut his earnings estimate for Staples' fiscal fourth quarter. Spellman didn't see the draft, which reached Staples' headquarters at 8:00 P.M., until 7:30 A.M. on the 20th. He tried unsuccessfully to reach Childe twice only to discover that the report had been released at 1:40 in the afternoon. Once again, Childe had given Staples no chance to respond to his extrapolations. And once again, the analyst began issuing reports asserting that his estimates were based on company "guidance," when in fact Staples had provided none.

Stemberg decided upon a new strategy. Not only would Staples cut off ongoing communication with Childe, it would no longer correct his drafts, even if he sent them. Stemberg did write to Stark, pointing out Childe's errors and noting that clients of Robertson Stephens & Co. who followed Childe's advice might not be faring well.

The summer of 1991 passed. The analyst continued to forecast weakening profit margins. By fall his dark outlook became more threatening. Childe again recommended selling Staples stock, but worse, had begun actively espousing his view in the media. In November, CNBC aired a story about Office Depot and Staples. It might as well have been called "Beauty and The Beast." According to the story, Office Depot was in a lovely position—essentially without any competitors invading its territory—while a big chunk of Staples' stores were about to suffer an assault from OfficeMax. Childe was not only referenced in the story, he seemed to be the only source for it.

Being wrong didn't seem to alter Childe's stance. He'd first recommended selling Staples short when it was at $13 per share. But the stock had continued to rise. Now, in early 1992, it was trading in the low 30s. Its astronomical P/E—now nearly 70—as well as Childe's constant refrain had attracted a number of short-sellers.

Staples' strategy of ignoring Childe and the shorts in order to focus on its business seemed like the best course until the next time the story hit the press. Stemberg was in court on a personal matter when Dan Dorfman, a columnist for *USA Today,* called for him. When Stemberg returned the call, Dorfman repeated the shorts' assertions: OfficeMax and Office Depot would soon be making inroads into Staples' kingdom in the Northeast, driving margins down. "I said, 'Look can I go off the record?' He said, 'Sure.' I said, 'We're going to bury the shorts and here's why . . .'" remembers Stemberg. The gist of the CEO's argument: OfficeMax would have more difficulty getting the real estate locations than they thought they would. And also, Staples' plan to lower prices would likely lead to greater market share.

After their conversation, Dorfman's March 30th column was a shock. "Pros: Staples to get hammered. CEO rails against critics." The story's first paragraph was even worse: "Repeatedly cursing and often speaking so fast I couldn't keep up with him, Tom Stemberg—43-year-old CEO of Staples, the country's second-largest chain of office-supply superstores—blasted his company's critics. 'They're so full of s—,' he says. 'I'm so [expletive] angry. It's outrageous what the [expletive] shorts are doing,'" wrote Dorfman. Childe was quoted saying, once again, that investors should sell Staples' stock.

"It was a vicious story. It made me look like a complete ass and buffoon," says Stemberg. Staples' requests for a correction were ignored, but history has borne out the company's confidence. By the end of fiscal 1992, same store sales were up 16 percent and Staples' stock rose to $33.50. (By the end of fiscal 1995, the stock had risen 124 percent above the 1992 level, adjusted for stock splits.) Childe eventually left Robertson Stephens & Co. And Dorfman, who left *USA Today* to become a columnist at *Money*, resigned from the magazine in 1996 because he refused to divulge his sources for other stories to *Money*'s editors.

Real-Life Lesson

Don't try to control what's out of your control. *You can—and should—build working relationships with analysts and reporters. But if they cannot be reasoned with—or flout the agreements you made with them—they are not worth your time. "When they cross the line, you've just got to let them know it," says Stemberg.*

Under Fire

Not all of the public controversy that Staples engendered revolved around its stock price. In the fall of 1994, the company inadvertently became center of a storm that erupted over Mitt Romney's campaign against Edward Kennedy for a U.S. Senate seat. Forty-seven-year-old Romney was an accomplished businessman, not a politician. As head of Bain Capital, he had backed Staples' crucial first round of private financing and by 1994 had invested $2.3 million in the company. In 1990, he temporarily returned to Bain & Co., the debt-ridden, floundering consulting firm for which he had once worked, to implement a successful turnaround. And though he is the son of George Romney, a three-term Republican governor of Michigan in the 1960s, his political heritage counted for nothing in Massachusetts, where the Kennedy name had been winning Senate seats on the Democratic ticket for thirty-two years.

It was a tough fight. The top three issues were crime, welfare, and jobs. With the election three months away, Romney began airing radio ads in which he claimed that he would be more effective at creating jobs than Kennedy. He had no record to support such a declaration in the political arena, of course, but ample evidence from his business career. The fast-growing companies in which Bain Capital had invested had added between ten thousand and seventeen thousand jobs. Staples, one of the premier success stories in Bain's portfolio of companies, was a key job-generator, having zoomed from zero to ten thousand employees in eight years. And Stemberg was an outspoken supporter of Romney, acting as cochair of the campaign finance committee and willingly granting interviews to the Boston reporters who called.

In the Kennedy campaign offices, Romney's remark about job creation smarted. The Democratic strategists soon revealed how they would counterattack. "In politics you look for anything to hit your opponent with," says Romney. "They looked at all eighty companies in which Bain Capital had invested and tried to find the most damaging thing they could." On September 15, Romney held a twenty-minute press conference in front of Staples' first store in Brighton. With him were the CEOs of some of the companies he had funded, including Stemberg and Judy George, founder of Domain, a furniture and accessories chain. The CEOs described how crucial Romney's support had been to their companies' success. A *Boston Globe* reporter lobbed an unexpected question at Stemberg: Did Staples offer its employees health insurance? Like most retailers, Staples offered health-care benefits to full-time employees, but not to part-timers, Stemberg told the reporter. When Romney took the microphone, he stressed the economic benefits of job creation. "I appreciate Ted Kennedy's years of service, but I don't think he has a clue to how to create jobs," he said. The *Globe* reporter later called Rick Gureghian, Kennedy's campaign spokesman, for a response to Romney's comment. According to an item in the next morning's *Globe*, Gureghian said, "Mitt Romney is pocketing millions of dollars creating service-industry, $4.50-an-hour part-time jobs that do not pay health insurance. And Mitt Romney thinks that's something to brag about?"

Stemberg was infuriated. But he got even hotter as he sat reading the newspaper in the kitchen of his country house in Marion, Massachusetts, the following morning. Saturday's paper contained a story describing Kennedy's plan to run a series of get-tough television ads that would expose the "real" Mitt Romney. "I said, 'Wait a minute.'

The theme is that these are bad jobs Romney helped create. It sounded like they would go on the air making false accusations," recalls Stemberg. He began calling around town and soon discovered that the advertisements did involve Staples.

Stemberg began a two-pronged campaign to straighten out the health benefits issue. The first step was to try to informally negotiate with Michael Kennedy, Kennedy's campaign manager. The second step was to formally complain. On the morning of September 19, Stemberg faxed a letter objecting to Gureghian's comment in the *Globe* to Kennedy's Washington, D.C., office. "These statements are flagrantly incorrect," he said. Moreover, the statements could damage the company's reputation and that of the two thousand Staples employees who were Massachusetts' residents, he pointed out. "You do represent them and their families, do you not?" There was dead silence from the Kennedy camp all day long.

Finally, at 10:00 P.M., out of the fax machine in Stemberg's home popped a two-page letter from Kennedy, the campaign manager. In it he asked eleven questions about Staples' wage and health benefits policies. "What contribution to coverage does Staples make to the cost of coverage for employees qualifying for coverage? Does this contribution vary among employees? If so, please describe the differences among salaried and hourly employees, low- and high-paid employees, more and less senior employees, etc." The clincher was that Kennedy wanted answers to these detailed questions by noon the next day. "If I do not hear from you by noon on Tuesday, September 20, 1994, I will assume that most of your employees do not receive health benefits through your company, and you can expect continued public discussion of these issues."

Stemberg decided to cut to the chase. Instead of filling

out the questionnaire that Kennedy had devised, he wrote a short letter containing two facts: Staples' entry-level wages exceeded $4.50 an hour and more than 50 percent of its employees received health benefits paid by the company. Though the Kennedy crew never publicly corrected their statements, they did refrain from using Staples name in the television ads.

Such facts surfaced but hardly seemed to matter amidst the avalanche of aggressive advertising mounted by Kennedy's well-oiled campaign machine. Romney lost. "My campaign was affected by the fact that I'm in business and that my opponents' campaign very skillfully took small features of our various investments and tried to make them into major events," concludes Romney.

Real-Life Lesson

Standing up for who you believe in isn't always pleasant. *One of the perks of success is that you and your company become better known and more influential. But a high profile makes you vulnerable as well as powerful. "Any time you take a stand, you take the chance that you're going to expose yourself to negative press," says Stemberg. It's part of the package, so don't be shocked when it happens.*

9 MISTAKES: REAL AND IMAGINED

The cliché is that in hindsight your vision is twenty-twenty. But even hindsight is a matter of perspective. Today you may think a five-year-old decision was a mistake. In another five years you may not. What we see as blunders only look that way because our view of the world has changed. Staples made its share of errors, all for what seemed like good reasons at the time. None was fatal, and some were actually helpful. Examine them together, though, and you see a road map of a gradually maturing business philosophy. Here are the missteps and what Staples' managers learned as a result of them.

Snaring Office Depot Some might argue that the most colossal error Staples made was not buying Office Depot, the Florida clone that grew faster, and became bigger, than Staples. Interestingly, Staples might not have had the chance to buy the company if not for a previous "mistake." The error? Allowing Fred Adler, one of Staples' venture capitalists, to indirectly back a rival office supply store chain—which turned out to be Office Depot—after he had invested in Staples. Within a year of Adler's "treasonous" act, his advisor, Joe Pagano, called Stemberg with some news: Pat Sher, Office Depot's founder, was dying of leukemia. The board was considering two options. No. 1: get another infusion of venture capital and bring in new management. Or No. 2, the action Pagano favored: merge Office Depot with Staples.

It was a great opportunity. Staples could leapfrog ahead of the sea of clones that had arisen in its wake, and do so with the second strongest company in the fledgling industry. But Stemberg felt torn. Office Depot was operating in a totally different part of the country, picking their store sites with a completely divergent strategy and—most worrisome—functioned with a "shoot 'em up" cowboy culture. After discussing the acquisition with Bob Leombruno, Paul Korian and Myra Hart, Stemberg decided to go for it. At best, he'd get the company. At worst, his interest would drive up the value of Office Depot, which would benefit Joe Pagano and, indirectly, Fred Adler. He told Adler he'd offer $12 million for the Florida company.

But the venture capitalists who controlled the company rejected Staples' offer. "Rather than selling out they wanted a bigger score. They wanted to go public as soon as possible," says Stemberg. He could have offered more money but he was nervous about managing Staples and Office Depot. "I was chicken," he recalls. "In those days they were a bunch of cowboys and they didn't want to sell to us. It would have been a difficult merger."

Real-Life Lesson

Be bold! *The merger undoubtedly would have been difficult, but would the merged company have failed? Probably not. Staples would have learned how to operate in nonurban settings much earlier than it did, and Office Depot would have learned how to study and refine its successes much sooner.*

Capturing Office Club While Stemberg let Office Depot slip away with few regrets, another missed chance filled him with anxiety for weeks. Once again, it involved Office Depot, as well as another rival, Office Club. In the fall of 1990, Stemberg ran into Office Club CEO Mark Begelman at Morton's Restaurant in Chicago, where both were attending the National Office Products Association convention. Begelman had spurned his former friend Stemberg ever since Staples entered the California market, which was Office Club's home turf. Stemberg asked Begelman about the rumors that Office Club was putting itself up for sale. Begelman confirmed them. His board had decided to sell the company, he said. Stemberg, who had always had a great deal of respect for Begelman, took the opportunity to apologize for the rupture in their friendship. Begelman seemed to accept it. Then Stemberg asked if they could talk about Staples acquiring Office Club. The two CEOs agreed to meet in Baltimore, Maryland, the following week, when both would be attending a conference sponsored by Alex Brown, a Baltimore brokerage firm.

Stemberg felt incredibly enthusiastic about buying Office Club. Combining Staples' stores with Office Club's would give it an unassailable position in California. Though Begelman seemed to welcome the idea of being acquired by Staples at their Maryland meeting, he called Stemberg in Framingham a week later to suggest that the discussions stop. Office Club's board would assess their options after the first of the year, he reported. So it was a complete shock to hear Begelman's message when Stemberg checked his voice mail at 8:00 A.M. one morning just before Christmas. "He said, 'Tom, I don't want you to read this in the newspaper, but you'll read it on the wire today. Today Office Depot acquired us,'" remembers Stemberg.

It was a devastating blow. Staples hadn't even been able

to throw its hat in the ring and make a proper bid for the company. And now Office Depot, Staples' biggest rival, had captured the prize. The acquisition would make Office Depot three times as large as Staples. "It was terrible," says Stemberg, who remembers wondering if Staples would end up as just another also-ran among a crowd of office supply companies. "I surely would never let on to many people, but it was one of the worst moments I've ever had in business."

Upon reflection, Stemberg understood why Office Depot was extraordinarily attractive to Begelman. The California executive could not only sell his company to the largest company in the industry, but because Office Depot had a vacant slot, he could become its president. There were other ties, as well. Begelman had lived in Florida and his wife was from the state. Office Club's venture capitalists were friendly with Office Depot's backers. The combination had personal and professional appeal.

Staples' response: Aggression. It quickly purchased ten California stores from HQ and stepped up the pace of store openings in Los Angeles. While the newly combined companies were in disarray, Staples focused like a laser beam upon the California market. It was the first in the industry to mount a dynamic advertising and promotional campaign—and it paid off. Within two years it had established a six-store edge and was by far the most recognized office supplies store name in Los Angeles. It wasn't revenge exactly—but it was just as sweet.

Real-Life Lesson

How you recover is more important than the mistakes you make. *Stunned as he was by Office Depot's new* strength, Stemberg was galvanized, too. He looked for the shred of opportunity in the bad news and found it: "We knew that Office Depot would have to reconcile two diverse concepts and real estate strategies. While they sorted it out, we could blow past them in Los Angeles," he says.

Small-Town Opportunities   In business, as in life, your outlook is irrevocably shaped by your origins. Because it started in the Northeast where the costs of doing business were extraordinarily high, Staples devised a strategy that would give it an advantage there: establish superstores that were smaller than most, to save on rent and operating costs, cluster them in densely populated areas, to justify paying for expensive advertisements, and stock the stores from a distribution center. Born of necessity, this is the strategy that would not only allow Staples to make a lot of money, but bar competitors from its turf.

It worked well, but Staples paid a price for the strategy's success: It couldn't see the potential in markets that didn't look like its home turf in the Northeast. Though Office Depot was planting stores willy-nilly, in towns with populations of just seventy-five thousand, Staples couldn't see how it could make money in small towns. "The numbers didn't work. We assumed that the trading area was ten or fifteen minutes and that our market share would be the same as it is in large cities," explains Stemberg. So for year after year, it focused on New York, Boston, and Los Angeles, where it knew the formula would work.

Then, in August of 1991, the company opened a store in Portland, Maine. With a population of two hundred thousand, the town was smaller than most of Staples' markets. But within months the store began doing extremely well. Customers were willing to drive much farther to get to the store, and because there was less competition, Staples' share of the local market grew to be much higher than in denser urban areas. Joe Vassalluzzo and John Wilson both believed that operating costs would be much lower in small towns than in cities and urged Stemberg to experiment. So in 1992 and 1993 Staples opened stores in places like Lancaster, Pennsylvania, and Victorville, California.

To their astonishment, the stores were total winners. They had not been able to make the numbers work because their most basic assumptions about a store's business were wrong when applied to a small town. Because the stores draw customers from farther away, small-town sales are almost as high as for big-city stores. Yet rent is half as much, merchandise shrinkage is half, and advertising costs are a fraction of what they would be in more populous areas. "Not going into small towns sooner was the dumbest thing we ever did," says Stemberg. "We were the last ones to move into them."

Real-Life Lesson

Sometimes rational analysis doesn't give you the right answers. *Intimate knowledge of your business can be an impediment as well as an advantage. If your assumptions are too fixed you won't be able to see that there may be multiple formulas for success. "Continuing to coldly go by the numbers isn't always the best course of action," says Stemberg. Be willing to experiment.*

Selling In New Ways Because they have to work so hard at bringing their vision to life, inventors of new business concepts can find it difficult to alter their idea. For Staples, the key mental stumbling block lay in the term *low-cost*. From its inception, Staples' appeal was low prices. To offer those low prices, Staples married a whole set of conditions. Its costs had to be low, so stores must be self-service and low on aesthetics. By definition, Staples' managers believed, their stores could not feature flocks of attentive clerks and pricey, attractive finishing touches.

One of the first challenges to this fixed definition was the customer who wanted delivery service. It was an obvious unfilled need. Customers were buying office supplies in bulk, as well as heavy items such as desks and file cabinets. They clearly wanted—and asked for—delivery. But taking its low-cost mission to heart, Staples' managers found plenty of reason to resist offering it. The question was, How many of its customers really would use this service? "We didn't want to add a lot of services because that would add cost to the business, and we didn't want to add cost to all of our customers to serve a few," explains Ron Sargent, president of Staples' Contract and Commercial division.

The board argued vehemently against offering delivery and mail order services. Their concern was that the delivery service could skew Staples business in such a way as to make it harder and harder to make a profit. "If it costs you $60 to pick and pack merchandise for a delivery, but you only charge $15 for it, then you've given that customer a $45 subsidy. The more your business moves in that direction, the less money you're going to make," says Stemberg. He was also worried that such a new service would dilute the company's efforts at growing its core business. But one by one, Staples' competitors offered delivery and mail order. More importantly, Staples' customers kept asking for the services.

So in 1988, Staples tested delivery and mail order in West Springfield, Massachusetts, and soon began rolling out the service throughout the chain. But it was a half-hearted effort. It did not go out of its way to let customers know that delivery was available. Its catalog was in black and white. And it penalized its best-potential customers for using delivery service. The charge for delivery was 5 percent of the order price. So a customer with a $300 order paid $15. A big spender with a $2,000 order paid $100. "What we were doing was discouraging big orders. Simple logic would say you want to give customers an incentive to have a big order," says Sargent.

But it was two or three years before Staples, after watching its competitors do well with the services, decided to look harder and more objectively at this nagging issue. Sargent, who was put in charge of the tiny operation, hired Bain Consulting to investigate the mail-order delivery business. The findings: Customers who ordered from a catalog were not necessarily the same ones who shopped in the stores. "There's a lot of cross-shopping that goes on between retail and mail-order customers. But the mail-order customer tends to be a little bigger and a little more interested in service. The customers in stores are more often buying for home offices," says Sargent. In other words, instead of cannibalizing Staples' basic business, the new services should be able to enlarge its customer base. "We could have done a better job understanding who our customer was," admits Stemberg.

Real-Life Lesson

There's more than one way to serve your customers. *When your strategy is working, nothing seems simpler than being very disciplined about executing it. That means not bending the rules. But sometimes a problem area, particularly* *one that is challenging your most basic assumptions, is pointing to a new way to provide customers what they want. If you can't see how to make that happen, advises Sargent, then get help. "We got outside help and we got help from other parts of Staples that had the expertise."*

10 GETTING BIGGER: TURNING WEAKNESSES INTO STRENGTHS

Recognizing that there was a segment of the business—delivery and mail-order—that Staples had treated like a stepchild was a significant insight. But deciding to mine the opportunity—and figuring out how to do it—were the really critical milestones. Staples' managers were forced to grapple with the question of whether or not to devote all their energies to expanding their core business, or to pioneer a new one. And the consequences of this decision would turn out to be much larger than any other time they had faced that quandary. From 1991 (when the company finally decided to set up the Contract and Commercial division as an independent unit) to 1995, the new business' sales grew from $30 million to $740 million. By the end of 1996, sales of the once-neglected business will probably exceed $1 billion—a level it took Staples itself nearly eight years to achieve.

One of the key events that led to Staples' decision to legitimize the mail-order business occurred in 1991 in the competitive California market. By then Office Depot, HQ, and Staples all had matching prices for delivery of merchandise: fifteen dollars or 5 percent of the order amount—whichever was more. What was significantly different about their delivery businesses was that Office Depot generated a good chunk of its California sales this

Ron Sargent

"When I got to Staples Direct, one of the first things I did was meet with every single employee in the call center, in groups of eight. It was interesting to hear the issues from their point of view. I mean, Tom said, 'Here are the issues.' And someone else said, 'Here are the issues.' It was incredible how different the priorities of the business are for people who are actually interacting with customers compared with senior management. We thought that we just didn't have a great marketing strategy. That's what I had heard. What the employees were saying was, 'There's no career path. I don't know what level I am. Some people are hired at $7 an hour and some people are hired at $8 an hour, and I've been here six months longer and I'm being paid $7 an hour.' It was basic employee relations issues. How could we expect them to up-sell and be nice to customers if they were so unhappy with their own job? Once you get that fixed then you can say, 'Okay, now, we've taken care of you. How do we take care of customers better?' It's not enough to have a great strategy, you need to address the people and the process of your business, too."

way, whereas Staples did relatively little. In mulling over the notion of changing to free delivery, Todd Krasnow realized that the modification could serve three important goals. First, if Staples offered free delivery, sales would rise considerably. Second, Staples would be the only one in the California market doing it—a competitive advantage that it could promote heavily. Finally, if and when Office Depot was forced to also offer free delivery, its margins would suffer, because it would be adding to the cost of business it was already doing. The strategy worked beautifully. And something unexpected happened. "We realized that as delivery volume went up, efficiency went up. Route density increased. Phone orders per order taker went up. So suddenly it was costing half as much—or less—to deliver. Instead of $20 per phone order, the cost of delivering fell to $9 per phone order," says Krasnow. As the economics changed, Staples realized this was a business opportunity worthy of attention.

But, odd as it sounds, plotting a course for the new business was especially difficult because of Staples' large size. Trying to grow a new, but complementary, venture in an established company is like trying to cultivate a seedling in a garden plot jammed with mature shrubs—the big sturdy plants just naturally soak up most of the sunshine, water, and fertilizer. That was apparent from day one, when Ron Sargent was installed as the head of Staples Direct, as the mail-order business was named. Because mail order had always been a sideshow to the main event, many parts of the business were not thought through.

After taking charge of the unit, Sargent interviewed the hundred or so employees who operated the call center. Though each of these workers constituted the sum total of a Staples shopping experience, at least for customers who only shopped by phone, they did not feel like an important part of the company. They were paid different rates per hour, for no clear reason, and had no idea how to progress in the organization. Sargent provided an ear, brought order to the compensation structure, and designed a career path. Sargent also had to cajole cooperation from Staples employees who were used to focusing on store sales, not catalog sales. Sargent's new unit had no distribution system of its own. So it had to rely on the system that served the stores—but, of course, it didn't carry the same clout.

The most difficult obstacle to overcome, however, was the sense of competition that grew between the stores and

Staples Direct. Because the store managers had always used the Staples catalog as a marketing tool, distributing it in the store and sending it to existing store customers, they were reluctant to give it up to the new unit. It felt like they were ceding control of their customers. Worse, they felt as though they got no credit when one of their customers placed a delivery order. "If a customer needs forty cases of copy paper, the easiest thing in world for a store associate to do is to tell the customer to call the 800 number. Instead you have situations where stores are saying, 'Well, I want to keep that sale in my store,'" says Sargent. Sharply divergent growth rates between the two areas reinforced the rivalry. Staples Direct's sales grew four times as fast as retail sales in 1995.

One by one, Sargent addressed these concerns. If a customer wanders into a store today and orders a desk to be delivered, the store gets credit for the sale, even though Staples Direct will pick, pack, and deliver the desk. What's more, a store's annual bonus is calculated, in part, by how well it has met its goals for generating delivery sales. The catalogs themselves are no longer filled with uninformative black-and-white line drawings of items. And though they are mailed to a vastly wider audience, existing store customers still receive them, too.

But the most significant change that stand-alone management brought to the mail-order and delivery business was a new lens through which to look at customers. With the help of Bain, Staples' board member Row Moriarty, and Tom Stemberg, Sargent analyzed who could be served by the new business. It was clear, from Staples' earlier experience, that most of its delivery customers were companies with up to fifty workers. But what hadn't been clear was that Staples could also serve two other customer categories: medium-sized businesses (with fifty to one hundred workers) and large ones (with more than a hundred). Looking out into the future, Sargent saw that if Staples built a separate system of distribution, merchandising, catalog operations, call centers, and other operations to support its delivery business, the company could leverage off of it to support sales to any size business—not just the smallish ones it had already hooked. So while the three segments would each have separate sales forces, the guts of their operations would be identical.

Figuring out this strategy up front allowed Staples to charge after its objectives in a much more focused and efficient way than simply letting the opportunity evolve. Because he was starting from scratch in trying to serve larger customers, Sargent embraced a growth-by-acquisition strategy. Staples had already dabbled with this by buying part of Eastman Stationers, a large contract stationer, in 1993. Though it acquired 16 percent of Eastman at a good price, Staples' co-owners wanted to resell the company quickly—and at a much higher price. "The equity value went from about $20 million to $80 million in three months," says Stemberg. In the end, Eastman's business was not strong enough to justify buying the rest of it at that price, Stemberg believed, so Staples passed. Eastman was sold to Office Depot instead.

Within two years, however, Staples has snapped up five regional stationers, and in February 1994 purchased National Office Supply, a contract stationer selling to *Fortune* 500 companies. Sargent's job quickly contained two contradictory imperatives: spur a fast-growing business while simultaneously consolidating and streamlining the acquired companies. Puzzling out the steps was so painful and complex that Sargent's Monday morning meeting with his eleven key managers came to be dubbed "Partners In Hell."

"You know that you're planning to have one group

that's going to buy product for our whole unit, and that group is going to be here, in Westborough, Massachusetts. But you can't have that buying group until, one, you move the right staff into Westborough, and two, we have a product line that's consistent throughout all of the acquired companies and our existing business. And we need to have computer and accounting systems that will support this consistent product line everywhere. It's kind of like a Rubik's cube," explains Sargent. "A year from now it's going to be a well-oiled machine, but we've got twelve months before we can say it's all integrated." Sargent has already made headway in reengineering the cost structure of the traditional contract stationer's business—with plans to extract 10 percentage points over next few years.

The fruits of this complex growth strategy are already apparent. By retaining the former owners of many of the acquired businesses, Staples has learned how to serve the *Fortune* 500 market faster than it otherwise would have—while at the same time holding onto key customers that it inherited through the acquisitions. "The companies that Staples acquired have been the cream of the crop. All of them have long-standing relationships with companies such as Xerox," says Henry Epstein, head of Staples Business Advantage who sold his regional contract business to Staples in 1994.

In return, Staples has brought nationwide name-brand recognition and sorely needed capital to the business. It has invested in a new management information system. It has helped develop cutting-edge software that will allow customers to order products through their computers. And it can custom-tailor a special feature at a customer's request. After wooing Ford for six months, National Office Supply (now Staples National Advantage) won the contract to provide the automaker with office supplies in

1991. But it wasn't until NOS's team of five had flown to Dearborn, Michigan, for a planning session that they learned Ford wanted to be able to pay for its purchases with a credit card. By channeling purchases through a credit card, the auto company would be able to minimize its accounts payable expenses, because the credit card company would handle all the paperwork. It was perfect for Ford—but no one at Staples knew it was part of their plan. Instead of waffling over the special request, the Staples team hustled to create a system that would accept credit cards in just ninety days. They made the deadline and realized they had devised a new marketing tool. "Once we had the system we were able to use it as a distinguishing feature from our competitors and implement it with customers like Pepsi Cola," says Evan Stern, the former president of National Office Supply who now heads Staples National Advantage.

Real-Life Lesson

From tiny pockets of neglect, mighty businesses can grow. *The disadvantage of launching a new enterprise in the middle of a fast-growing profitable business is that it gets no respect. The advantage, though, is that once that new enterprise finds sponsorship, it can aim very high because it has the resources it needs. Don't let an afterthought to your main business be ignored for too long without thoroughly analyzing its potential.*

Shedding Skins: Make Way for the New

The challenges of growing from a $3 billion company to a $10 billion company, which Staples plans to do by the turn of the century, are many. But one of the most important is symbolized by a vigorous, lengthy debate over an apparently simple matter: should Staples' stores feature concrete or tile floors? It sounds laughable. But it was, in fact, a pivotal issue. Because it showed that Staples couldn't grow in crucial ways until the organization was willing to shed old beliefs, old habits, and old paradigms. Making way for the new meant tossing out outgrown or outmoded notions.

But that is extremely tough to do. Concrete floors in stores signified a whole set of associations. Warehouse stores have concrete floors because they are inexpensive to install and to maintain. When Stemberg started Staples he was emulating warehouse stores, with their low prices, so he opted for concrete floors. Silly as it sounds, concrete floors seemed as much a part of Staples' success as low prices because they were all wrapped up in the original set of beliefs that created the office supply superstore concept.

But when Jack Bingleman joined Staples in 1994, after the company acquired the rest of his Canadian store chain, he brought a new set of beliefs: low prices could coexist with a brighter, more aesthetically appealing store. "I felt that the stores, from the standpoint of Staples' customers, had become dull and unexciting. I felt that customers deserved a much more exciting and customer-friendly shopping experience," says Bingleman.

His proposal was dramatic: redesign new stores to be larger and undertake a massive remodeling of the old stores. It was going to be incredibly expensive. And, in some ways, it seemed a frivolous expenditure when Staples was still building new stores at a frantic pace. To change

Jack Bingleman

"For the longest time Staples resisted the fact that consumers, not just small businesses, came to the stores. We always said that we wanted to have small business people shop at our stores, which would have included somebody that runs a business from their home. But there's no such thing as the average situation. A home business can be anything from a serious, paper-intensive operation to a real estate agent to a retired person working on investments. While we were born to look after people who were running a business, over time it became clear that we were just the perfect place for students and teachers and consumers and others to come to. And then, when we saw how people came to us for office supplies, it was a natural that they would come to us for business machines. It isn't very long before you realize that there are more consumer computer-and-software buyers than there are business buyers. The same with office furniture. You could have sat there and said, 'No. The business customer is the only one we're interested in.' But we evolved."

the Staples' definition of a Staples store, Bingleman had to introduce a new standard of measure. They should not judge the stores on the basis of improvements already made, but on the basis of what the customer saw. "How did they look when you walked in the front door? How easily could you move around the store? Were we really doing a great job of buying regular and promotional and new forward-thinking, high-technology merchandise that really turned the customer on?" asked Bingleman.

His view finally prevailed. Remodeled stores are crisp and bright. Customers are no longer forced to move through the store in the way they used to be. You can buy more items that are new on the market . . . and the floors are tile. The decision has been validated by dollars and cents, too. Customers' response to renovated stores has been twice as good as the average retail remodeling gets.

Real-Life Lesson

Growth hurts. *It's scary to give up ideas that have made you a success. But you've probably outgrown some of them. Or the marketplace has rendered them obsolete. You and your organization can't move to a new level unless you jettison that baggage.*

Building an Organization: The Guts of a New Machine

After sawing off old, outmoded ideas, with what do you replace them? What's the bridge from a $3 billion company to a $10 billion giant? When it confronted that question late in 1994, Staples executives decided the answer had two components: a customer-oriented culture and the systems of a $10 billion company.

Marty Hanaka, a 20-year veteran of Sears Roebuck who joined the company as president and chief operating officer in 1994, believes that to get to the big leagues, every single employee's level of consciousness has to be raised. "The old days of putting together a seventeen thousand square foot store with the grocery store approach to basic assortments and letting a customer pick and choose, fill up a basket, and check out was probably fine at one time. To compete and win in the future we have to change from a pure operating company to one that is more customer service-oriented and sales-oriented," he asserts.

It's the kind of pronouncement that makes the rank-and-file roll their eyes. Even at Staples, workers had heard it before. To make the transformation work, the Staples executives began folding a customer-driven perspective into a multitude of efforts. First came the touchy-feely part: drafting a mission statement of the values Staples should embrace and embody. Stemberg and Hanaka asked each operational area of the company to contribute one of their best people to form a task force that would have credibility within the organization. The group's final statement of values was CARE, an acronym for four areas of focus: customers, associates (Staples employees), real communications, and execution.

Rather than kick off the new mission with a 3-x-5

Todd Krasnow

"Opening and running one store is very different from having ten stores. When you go from one store to ten stores you suddenly have to worry about systems: for hiring people; for getting the payroll done properly; for ordering your product and making sure all the stores are replenished properly. You can no longer do these things by hand. Then, when you get to be one hundred stores, you need to worry about inventory control and shrink, issues that you didn't worry about before. The requirement for information systems changes radically as the business grows. It sure would be nice if somebody would periodically have said, 'Okay, everybody. Time out! Now, we've got to change.' But nobody knew enough to do that. You're just puzzling it all out as you go. You have an idea of what the company's various systems should eventually look like. But you don't know for sure."

card in everyone's pay envelope, Hanaka and the task force, starting in 1995, have tried to embed it throughout operations. It is built into the company's mystery shopping program, to see how thoroughly stores embrace the values. Customer compliments and complaints are categorized by company function, so that each area of the company knows how it is faring in meeting customers needs. The company formed a customer satisfaction group, which has been charged with accumulating data in order to correct problems at the root cause as well as anticipate trends.

Similarly, employees are measured and rewarded on the basis of how well they meet the standards espoused in the CARE mission statement. That standard, in fact, determines success more than job titles. "We're trying to create an organization and a workplace where we get the highest and best use of everybody. I don't mean this in a corny or superficial sense, but we want an aligned, functioning team where it doesn't matter what job or title you have ... where what matters is winning as a company," says Hanaka. And if the company *does* win, in terms of profits, then so do Staples employees. Most employees get a chance to own the company's stock through various plans.

In addition to transforming Staples' culture, the other large-scale change required before Staples can reach its $10 billion goal is to acquire the infrastructure—everything from technology to job slots—to support operations on such a scale. For years, Staples' top managers could depend on simple proximity to stay abreast of all developments in the company. But by 1994, the company had grown much too large for that casual approach. So in 1995, Hanaka called for the formation of a "point team" of seven key managers. "We're trying to create a method where there's regular communication, sharing of goals, alignment on policy issues and decisions. While we can disagree privately, we're going to be one cohesive, unified group to the organization," explains Hanaka.

Thinking on a different scale requires hiring in advance of truly needing a certain position. In finance, for example, CFO John Wilson has created three or four positions that simply did not exist before because one person could handle all the tasks. Having separate people handle tax planning, investor relations, treasury, and controller functions is crucial not only because those jobs will become more time-intensive as the company grows, but, if they are well-executed, they will have a huge impact on the bottom line. "When you're a $4 or $5 billion company, a 10–basis point improvement in this or that area becomes a very large number in extra profits," says Wilson.

One area in which anticipating fast growth has helped

Staples to achieve a competitive advantage: technology and information systems. Though analyzing and implementing new computer systems so frequently has been taxing, Staples workers get to use state-of-the-art systems. "Because they've had their systems so long, some of the old retailers can't really incorporate new developments. We're able to buy the best of the improvements and make the transition with limited expense," explains Wilson. The trick of getting increasing returns out of every small improvement is what will catapult not just Staples' information systems, but its entire organization, into the realm of the giants.

Real-Life Lesson

Becoming a disciplined giant requires new disciplines. *When your business is small, you don't need to think twice about your company's culture or philosophy. A common interest knits everyone together. But as your company grows, its sheer scale causes common interests to splinter. Managers can't single-handedly overcome that trend. Your principles and values need to be embedded in the company's systems to become consistent throughout.*

11 LESSONS LEARNED: A PERSONAL JOURNEY

Being an entrepreneur is a way of seeing into the future. For Tom Stemberg, in the beginning that meant envisioning a store that did not yet exist. As Staples grew, it meant enlarging the lens to encompass broader markets and varying strategies. Today it means foreseeing the engines of growth that will catapult Staples into the next century as a $10 billion juggernaut. Performing this forward thinking, while at the same time solving everyday business problems, is the first trick a company founder must learn—and one of the most useful at any stage of a company's growth. "You have to live reality, but dream the dream," says Stemberg.

But what does a company founder see when he looks backward? This book has mostly focused on real-life lessons that fledgling and established companies can draw from Staples' first, action-packed decade of life. But none of those truths could have emerged if Stemberg himself had not embarked on his own journey of learning and evolution. What became reality first started inside his head. Looking back, Stemberg recognizes that his personal odyssey has taught him personal truths that have been even more essential than the corporate lessons. Here's what he's learned.

Never Underestimate the Potential of What You Are Doing

There's no shortage of forces that conspire to minimize your dream, to suggest that failure is the probable outcome. Like Darth Vader luring Luke Skywalker over to the "dark side," new competitors, experienced experts, even the status quo collaborate against someone who is trying to do something new. Overcoming the siren call of failure is one reason never to sell your idea short.

The second reason is that, once you have begun, your idea will probably carry you much further than you expected. As Goethe said, "What you can do, or dream you can, begin it. Boldness has genius, power, and magic in it." Time and again, Stemberg found he underestimated how large and deep the U.S. market for office supplies would be. When he first started the company, his business plan estimated that the industry he was creating would be $80 million.

By 1990, he knew better—Staples itself had surpassed that sales level, and it had sizable competitors in the industry. The real limit, he thought at that point, was $1 billion. It was a much bigger number, but not so big that Stemberg felt he could ignore its significance: Staples and its competitors would soon saturate the North American market, he thought. The company had better act quickly to find business opportunities that would allow it to keep revenues growing rapidly. "We were just very concerned that we would run out of room to grow," he remembers. That is when Staples embarked on its two joint ventures in Europe.

Amazingly, the core appetite for Staples' expertise just continued to grow. The ranks of the self-employed and at-home workers swelled. The nonbusiness consumer was increasingly attracted to Staples stores. And Staples finally discovered the unique rewards of serving small towns. Together these developments moved back the point at which the company will simply be unable to find another corner in which to park a store. "Here we are, six years after I worried about running out of room, and we are opening 120 stores a year. We are no where near the end of growth in North American profitability," says Tom. The new target: There will be close to three thousand stores in North America before the market is saturated. As of the beginning of 1996, there were less than half that many.

To See the Positive in a Sea of Bad News

If the defining characteristic of an entrepreneur is to see into the future, his defining bias is to see opportunity in every setback. For Stemberg, the entrepreneurial sense of optimism was best described by a joke that Bryant Gumbel, the NBC morning show anchor, told him at a Friends of Harvard Basketball banquet. It's Christmas morning and two kids—one a pessimist, the other an optimist—open their presents. The pessimist gets a brand-new bike decked out with decals and accessories in the latest style. "It looks great," he says. "But it'll probably break soon." The second kid, an optimist, opens up a huge package, finds it filled with horse manure and jumps with glee, exclaiming, "There must be a pony in there somewhere!"

Stemberg has regularly called upon his ability to wrestle good out of adversity. Two stores that lost money for Finast, his former employer, are now profitable Staples stores. The Northeast, Staples' launching spot, was filled with extraordinary drawbacks: high labor, rental, and advertising costs. But Stemberg turned those disadvantages into advantages by designing his superstores to be small and building enough of them to keep out competitors and justify advertising. The unforeseen bonus to this approach: "Now we are enjoying the easy sailing of small towns like Keaneck and Muskegon and Ocala," says Stemberg.

When Henry Nasella, the company's chief operating officer quit, in 1993, Stemberg could have—and by some observers' reckoning, *should* have—wrung his hands. As the former president of Star Markets and Staples' day-to-day business manager, Nasella had a hands-on operator's credibility and had won the confidence of Wall Street investors. Without Nasella, Wall Street analysts fretted, Staples might come unglued. But Stemberg did not see it that way. "Instead I saw it as an opportunity to position the management that could take Staples to the next level and the next century," he says.

Lead by Example

This is probably the toughest rule to follow because it requires self-monitoring, self-control, and, most important, constantly reinventing yourself. Leading by example was pretty easy, in the beginning. When Staples started there were so few employees and every one of them was so intensely involved in the same effort, that it was natural to absorb similar values and priorities. But as the company grew larger, what was valued became murkier, more open to interpretation. And too often employees mistake what the CEO likes for what is best for the company. "When word gets out that the chairman likes coffee, the next thing you know the staff buys Nicaragua," says Stemberg, paraphrasing a comment by Bernie Marcus, founder and CEO of Home Depot, at a *Fortune* magazine seminar.

The antidote to bureaucracy and politics, Stemberg believes, is to resist the easy answers and search for a true picture of your business. "When you get larger, more and more people tell you what you want to hear as opposed to the truth," says Stemberg. He stays close to the guts of his operation by spending at least a day a week on the front lines, visiting stores, call centers, and distribution facilities. "The more unfiltered truth I hear, the better." He also encourages risk-taking by rewarding managers who spot problems or take on controversial issues. "If you want people to try things, then you'd better create an atmosphere where you encourage it," explains Stemberg. "Don't ream them after the fact if they try something gutsy and it doesn't work."

The most sophisticated way to lead is often the hardest for an entrepreneur, who is by definition a hands-on doer. It requires establishing the company's values and principles, and then stepping back to let others implement them. The man of action must become the man behind the curtain. It is a transition many entrepreneurs never pull off. But it is the most rewarding of all accomplishments. "What you really want to do is set in place principles and the broad outline of your objectives. But you don't want to worry about whether an innovation is your idea or somebody else's. One of my frustrations is when a member of my management team is striving for recognition and insists on getting credit for something. They forget that it's much better to make it their peoples' idea," says Stemberg. "The most gratifying thing in the world is if your people do something exactly the way you hoped—arguably better than you would have done it yourself—without you having to tell them to. That's the greatest feeling in the world."

INDEX

Adler, Fred *34, 36, 56–58, 115, 116*
Alex Brown *117*
Allied Office Supply *9*
American Stores *13, 46*
American Stores Co. *46*
American Stores Properties Inc. *46*
Ampad *18*
AT&T *28*

Bain & Co. *110*
Bain Capital *33, 39, 110, 111*
Bain Consulting *33, 122*
Balter, Gary *100*
Bauer, Michael *87*
Beaver Lumber *78, 94*
Begelman, Mark *89*
Berg, John *98, 99, 102, 103*
Berkowitz, Alan *69*
Bessemer Securities *18*
Bingleman, Jack *78–81, 94–96, 132, 133*
Black, Conrad *94*
Blair Ventures *40*
Boise Cascade *7, 12*
Burton, Betsy *69*
Business Depot *80, 81, 94–96*

Charles River Venture Partners *32*
Cheadle, Bo *58, 59, 98*
Childe, David *106–109*
Citicorp *40*
Cohrs, Michael *102*
Computer City *49*
Contract and Commercial division, Staples' *47, 121, 125*
Cormier, Ed *27, 28*
Coven, Danny *26*

Dart Drug *103*
Delaware Management *101*
Domain *111*
Dominion stores *94*
Donaldson, Lufkin and Jenrette *32*
Dorfman, Dan *108, 109*
Dougherty, Steve *92, 96*
Downer & Co. *25, 32*

Eastman Stationers *129*
Edwards Supermarkets *27*
Edwards-Finast division *3, 4*
Epstein, Henry *130*
Esseltes *18*

Fidelity *98*
Finn, Una *69*
First National Supermarkets *1, 3, 14, 27*
Flieck, Henry *46, 51, 75*
Ford *130, 131*
Frahm, Barry *39*
Fretters *49*
Fuente, David *92, 93*

George, Judy *111*
Gillette *18*
Globus *95*
Goldberg, Al *71, 72*
Goldman Sachs *38, 80, 99–101*
Gramaglia, Suzanne *69*
Great Canadian Office Supply Warehouse *95*
Grossman's Lumber *38, 56*
Grossman, Mike *38, 56, 78*
Gumbel, Bryant *142*
Gureghian, Rick *111, 112*

Index

Haft, Bobby *103*
Hambro *34, 39*
Hanaka, Marty *135–137*
Hardymon, Felda *33, 35, 57*
Hart, Myra *12, 14–17, 21, 22, 27, 28, 42, 71, 72, 116*
Heisey, Larry *69*
Highland Superstores 51
Home Depot *3, 37, 56, 78, 144*
Hughes, John *69*
HQ International *59*
HQ Office Supplies Warehouse *59, 97*

IKEA *87*
Intelligent Electronics *43*
International Paper *18*

Jewel Companies *2, 28*

Kahn, Leo *2, 4, 6, 16, 26, 28, 31, 32, 68, 69, 71, 72*
Kemper *98*
Kennedy, Edward *110–113*
Kennedy, Larry *18*
Kennedy, Michael *112*
Kingfisher, plc. *83*
Kings department stores *16*
Kmart *55*
Korian, Paul *13, 15, 18, 19, 116*
Krasnow, Todd *15, 16, 18, 22–24, 61, 62, 64, 85*

Lazarus, Charles *55*
le Fort, Peter von *87*
Leombruno, Bob *13, 15, 17, 18, 37, 38, 99, 116*
Levy, Coleman *6*
Lubrano, Dave *29, 35, 69, 79, 98*

Makro *4, 5*
Mammoth Mart *13*
Marcus, Bernie *144*

Margolius, Ralph *9*
Marx, Ralph *72*
Mast Industries *39*
Max Bahr *87*
MAXI-Papier *85–87*
McArthur, John *29*
McGlade, Katherine *75*
Meadow, Scott *31*
Mercury Warburg *102*
Mintz and Hoke Advertising *14*
Molsen *78*
Montgomery Securities *58, 59, 98*
Montgomery Ward *63*
Moody, Jim *69*
Moriarty, Row *69, 128*
Mr. How *56*
MVP Sports *49*

Naisbitt, John *8*
Nakasone, Bob *6, 28, 29, 55, 69*
Nasella, Henry *142*
National Office Products Association *18, 92, 117*
National Office Supply *129–131*

O Henry *39*
Office Club *59, 61, 65, 66, 78, 89–91, 97, 117, 118*
Office Depot *37, 50, 51, 56–59, 61–66*
Office Place *59*
Office Stop *50*
Office Warehouse *65*
Office World *59, 63*
OfficeMax *51, 52, 82, 108*
Osco Drug (American Stores) *13*

Pacey, Larry *65*
Pagano, Joe *57, 115, 116*
Parneros, Demos *69*
Patrick, Ian *12, 13*

Pellerin, Wallace *10*
Perkins, Don *28*
Poma, Ricardo *39*
Price Club *61, 89–91, 103*
Purity Supreme *2, 28*

Reilly, Bob *25, 32*
Robertson Stephens & Co. *106, 108, 109*
Romney, Mitt *33, 34, 39, 57, 69, 110–113*

Salmon, Walter *4, 27*
Samuels, Sandy *34*
Sargent, Ron *42, 44, 45, 47, 121-123, 126–130*
Sears Roebuck *135*
Securities and Exchange Commission *100*
Security Pacific *40*
Sethness, Chuck *29*
Sher, Pat *56, 115*
Spellman, Bob *102, 107*
Sprout Group, The *32*
Staples Business Advantage *130*
Staples Direct *29, 55, 126–128*
Staples National Advantage *130, 131*
Star Markets *2, 12, 15, 27, 142*
Stark, Michael *107, 108*
Starr, Dinny *69*
State Street Research *98*
Stern, Evan *131*
Superior Brands *29, 35*
Supermarkets General *4*

Texas Business Products *10*
Time *28*
Toys "R" Us *3, 5, 6, 10, 28, 33, 39, 57*
Trust, Marty *39, 40, 69*

USAir *103*

Vassalluzzo, Joe *42–46, 48–50*

Wal-Mart *55, 56*
Walsh, Paul *69*
Wasserman, Phyllis *96*
Weld, Bill *69*
Westerfield, Steve *42, 66, 80, 82, 92–96*
Wholesale Stationers Association *39*
Willliam Blair *31, 99*
Wilson, John *102, 104–106, 120, 137, 138*
Woolworth *83*
WORKplace *42, 59, 66, 92–94, 96*

Xerox *12, 130*